500 Earrings

500 EARRINGS

NEW DIRECTIONS IN CONTEMPORARY JEWELRY

LARK BOOKS

A Division of
Sterling Publishing Co., Inc.
New York

EDITOR: **Marthe Le Van**

ART DIRECTOR: **Matt Shay, Shay Design**

COVER DESIGNER: **Barbara Zaretsky,
Cindy LaBreacht**

ASSOCIATE EDITOR: **Nathalie Mornu**

ASSOCIATE ART DIRECTOR: **Lance Wille,
Shannon Yokeley**

ART PRODUCTION ASSISTANT: **Jeff Hamilton**

ADMINISTRATIVE ASSISTANT: **Dawn Dillingham,
Rosemary Kast**

EDITORIAL INTERNS: **Janet Hurley,
Katrina Usher**

PROOFREADER: **Jessica Boing**

COVER:
Todd Reed
Untitled, 2004

SPINE:
Giselle Kolb
Earrings, 2005

BACK COVER, TOP:
Sasha Samuels
Black and Whites, 1995

BACK COVER, BOTTOM LEFT:
Tami Dean
Glitz Kick Earrings, 2006

BACK COVER, BOTTOM CENTER:
Chih-Wen Chiu
Variety, 2004

BACK COVER, BOTTOM RIGHT:
Carol Webb
Half Torii #7, 1995

FRONT FLAP:
Beth Rosengard
Neon Dusters, 2005

BACK FLAP:
Luana Coonen
Morpho Encasements, 2005

TITLE PAGE:
Ellen Himic
Slide and Snap Earrings, 2006

FACING PAGE:
Jessica Scofield
Trellis Earrings, 2006

Library of Congress Cataloging-in-Publication Data

500 earrings : new directions in contemporary jewelry.
    p. cm.
  Includes index.
  ISBN 1-57990-823-3 (pbk.)
  1. Jewelry making. 2. Earrings. I. Title: Five hundred earrings.
  TT212.A143 2007
  745.594'2--dc22

                                      2006031140

10 9 8 7 6 5 4 3 2 1

First Edition

Published by Lark Books, A Division of
Sterling Publishing Co., Inc.
387 Park Avenue South, New York, N.Y. 10016

Text © 2007, Lark Books
Photography © Artist/Photographer

Distributed in Canada by Sterling Publishing,
c/o Canadian Manda Group, 165 Dufferin Street
Toronto, Ontario, Canada M6K 3H6

Distributed in the United Kingdom by GMC Distribution Services,
Castle Place, 166 High Street, Lewes, East Sussex, England BN7 1XU

Distributed in Australia by Capricorn Link (Australia) Pty Ltd.,
P.O. Box 704, Windsor, NSW 2756 Australia

If you have questions or comments about this book, please contact:
Lark Books
67 Broadway
Asheville, NC 28801
(828) 253-0467

Manufactured in China

ISBN 13: 978-1-57990-823-2
ISBN 10: 1-57990-823-3

For information about custom editions, special sales, premium and corporate
purchases, please contact Sterling Special Sales Department at 800-805-5489
or specialsales@sterlingpub.com.

Contents

Introduction by Alan Revere, Juror   6

The Earrings   8

Contributing Artists   406

Acknowledgments   408

Catherine Clark Gilbertson
Earpiece #1 | 2003

Annette Ehinger
Unique Pieces | 2006

Introduction

I have an affinity for earrings, which may sound funny for a bearded man who has never worn one. But it's true. I designed my first pair of platinum, diamond, and ruby earrings when I was 10 years old! My mother took me to 47th Street, the jewelry district in New York, where the family jeweler and I redesigned some pieces from my grandmother into a pair of kinetic earrings with dangling rubies for my mother. I had no idea how significant that day would be. I inherited those earrings and earrings then became the main vehicle for my creativity as a full-time jewelry designer and maker.

Earrings were among the first pieces I ever made. On page 296 is a pair I designed and fabricated in 1973 with two kinetic movements. Over a period of 20 years, I created hundreds of original earring designs, and my small team of bench jewelers handcrafted thousands of pairs in gold and silver. During those years, my work won many awards, nearly all for earring designs.

Earrings are my favorite form of jewelry for a number of reasons. They are the most sculptural jewelry expression with unlimited possibilities for design. Earrings are often suspended so that they are visible from all sides, as well as from above and below. Almost anything can be hung onto or dangled from an ear, as evidenced by Stacy Petersen's *Branches* (page 382). Earrings are not limited by the size of the wearer, as are bracelets and rings. While most earring forms are specific to the ear, there are exceptions. Earrings often, but not always, come in pairs. They are often, but not always, matching. The proximity to the face makes earrings highly visible; one has to look harder to find pendants—which are often covered by shirts or jackets—or rings, which can be small and hard to spot on someone's hand.

Earrings have unique physical characteristics and requirements that compel designers to ask many questions. Will the earring hug the ear or dangle? Will it hang straight with gravity? Will it be light enough to wear comfortably? Will it use a conventional post and clutch, or a hook, or neither? Will it sit up on the earlobe and cover the hole or will it be suspended and expose the lobe? How long will it be: moderate, long, down to the shoulder, down to the waist? Will it be stationary or moving? The answers make earrings the most dramatic and playful of all jewelry forms and they often come to life with the wearer's movements.

Women own and wear far more pairs of earrings than other types of jewelry. Through personal conversations with my customers, I learned that earrings are perceived as "less serious" than necklaces, brooches, or bracelets. They are less likely to carry the social significance of rings. Gold and silver earrings are usually lighter, made from less metal, and, therefore more affordable than bracelets or necklaces. Earrings are an essential fashion accessory and are coordinated with apparel more often than other jewelry.

I established some basic criteria to guide me through the wonderful and daunting task of selecting 500 earrings from over 2,500 submissions. First, the work had to appear well crafted: solder seams had to be clean and uninterrupted, polish and finish had to be even and deliberate with no tool marks or sloppy workmanship. I did make some exceptions for pieces where other qualities of design far outweighed these considerations or where a more crude appearance was obviously a design element. I looked for examples of key metalworking techniques—forging, fabrication, granulation, or casting—and for exotic, new, or alternative techniques like mokume gane, anticlastic forming, fold forming, kum boo.

Next, I sought interesting or unusual forms, concepts and presentations across media. For example, Françoise and Claude Chavent created a clever and successful trompe l'oeil effect in their work, *Cubes* (page 169) and *Copeaux*. These earrings are both totally flat despite appearing to have volume. In *Unique Pieces*, Annette Ehinger left a rough handle of stone at the top of each sophisticated, faceted amethyst and then used a simple twist of gold wire to hold it to the ear. Other artists effectively reimagined and repurposed nontraditional materials, such as toothpicks, coffee filters, candy, grass, feathers, and shells.

If the work displayed commitment and passion, I then looked for any of a number of additional qualities such as innovation (see Catherine Clark Gilbertson's *Earpiece #1*), humor, tradition, emotion, narration (see Noriko Sugawara's *Dreams*), interaction, composition, surprise, and of course—beauty. Chi Yu-Fang's *Laced with Lace I* (page 238) is an example of femininity, beauty, innovation, physicality, sensuality, and surprise combined.

As the juror for *500 Earrings*, I was pleased to find a collection of work that captures current trends in contemporary jewelry: exploration of materials, innovative methods, and contemplative solutions alongside a traditional search for beauty. I concluded that the term "earrings" is really a poor choice to describe what is in this book. The concept of a ring passing through an earlobe represents a small fraction of the jewelry on the following pages. In other languages, there are words that mean ear ornament, ear hangers, ear wear, ear holders, and ear attachments. But in English, we are stuck with "earrings," so this term will have to suffice. Regardless of the terminology, this collection pushed me to step outside another box, expanding my own understanding of how and what artists can hang on a human ear—which is a long way from my beginnings on 47th Street.

Alan Revere

Noriko Sugawara
Dreams | 2004

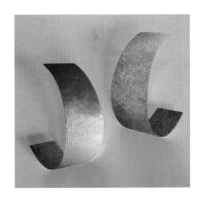

Françoise and Claude Chavent
Copeaux | 2005

Michael Good
Untitled | 2000

EACH, 3.2 CM IN DIAMETER

18-karat gold; hand formed, anticlastic
raising, polished, sandblasted

PHOTO BY PAM MARRACINI

Noriko Sugawara
Morning Dew | 2004
EACH, 3 X 3 X 1 CM
18-karat gold, moonstones,
diamonds; hand fabricated
PHOTO BY RALPH GABRINER

Jacqueline Ryan
Untitled | 2002

EACH, 2.6 X 2.6 X 0.8 CM

18-karat gold; hand pierced,
forged, soldered

PHOTO BY GIOVANNI CORVAJA
COURTESY OF CHARON KRANSEN ARTS,
NEW YORK, NEW YORK

Natasha Wozniak
Wish-Fulfilling Vine Earrings | 2004
EACH, 5 X 1.6 X 1 CM
18-karat gold, 22-karat gold, tourmalines;
repoussé, cut, soldered, bezel set
PHOTO BY RALPH GABRINER

Annamaria Zanella
Boxes | 2002
3 X 3 X 1 CM
22-karat gold; hand fabricated
PHOTO BY GIULIO RUSTICHELLI

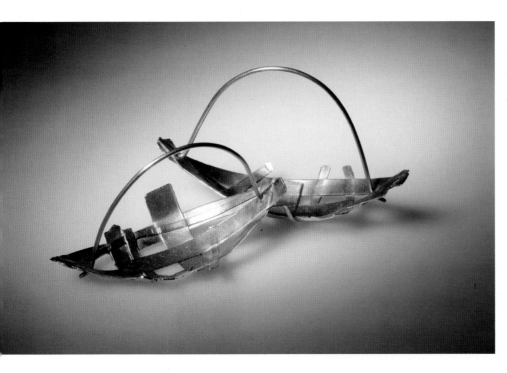

Mareen Alburg
Boats Silver | 2004
EACH, 5 X 6 X 2 CM
Sterling silver,
gold plate; cast
PHOTO BY ARTIST

Jerry Scavezze
Trio | 2005
EACH, 2.5 X 1 X 0.5 CM
14-karat gold, diamonds; anticlastic
forming, torqued, assembled

With this piece we are moving anticlastic forming from monoshell forms into multi-element forms. JERRY SCAVEZZE

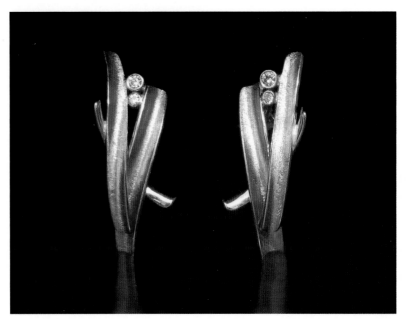

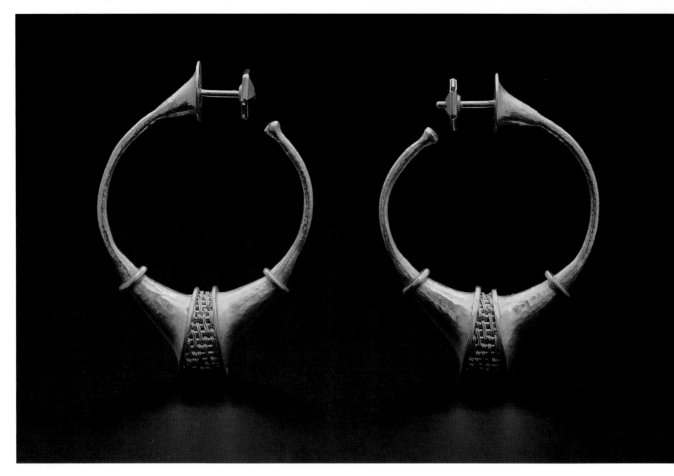

Mary Lee Hu
Earrings # 126 | 1988
EACH, 4.5 X 3.3 X 1.5 CM
18-karat gold, 22-karat gold;
twined, forged, fabricated
PHOTO BY RICHARD NICOL

Giovanni Corvaja
Untitled | 1999
EACH, 3 X 1.5 X 0.9 CM
22-karat gold; niello
PHOTO BY ARTIST

Noriko Sugawara

Dreams | 2004

EACH, 5 X 0.8 X 0.5 CM

24-karat gold, 18-karat gold, shakudo, diamonds, Japanese patina; hand fabricated, inlay, cast

PHOTO BY KOICHIRO SHIIKI

Jayne Redman
Tulip Earrings | 2001
EACH, 4.2 X 2 X 2 CM
18-karat yellow gold, fine silver;
hand fabricated, kum boo, oxidized
PHOTO BY ROBERT DIAMANTE

Mark Kanazawa

Untitled | 2006

EACH, 5.5 X 3 X 0.3 CM

Sterling silver, 14-karat gold;
hand fabricated, oxidized

PHOTO BY GUY NICOL

Sharon Massey
Temple Bell Earrings | 2005
LONGEST, 8 X 1 X 1 CM
Sterling silver, 24-karat gold; hand
fabricated, kum boo, oxidized
PHOTO BY ROBERT DIAMANTE

Sondra Sherman

Chandeliers for the Ears | 1990

LARGEST, 6 X 2.5 CM

Sterling silver, 18-karat gold plate,
glass button

PHOTO BY JOCHEN GERZ

Rob Jackson
Diamond Earrings | 2000
EACH, 3.2 X 1.2 X 0.5 CM
Iron nail fragments, 18-karat gold,
diamonds; hand fabricated
PHOTO BY ARTIST

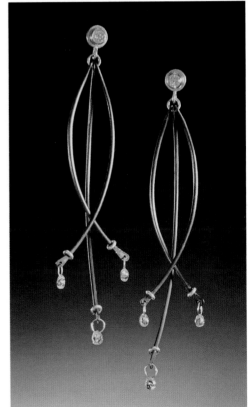

Karen Mitchell, Karen Mitchell Design
Untitled | 2005
EACH, 8 X 3.5 CM
22-karat gold, diamonds, blackened steel
PHOTO BY RALPH GABRINER

Christine Uemura

Avian Mécanique | 2006

EACH, 7 X 3.2 X 0.5 CM

22-karat gold, sterling silver;
hand fabricated, riveted

PHOTO BY GEORGE POST

The weight of the eggs hanging below causes the bird to flap its wings when the wearer moves. Jewelry can be dynamic; it can reflect the energy of our bodies. CHRISTINE UEMURA

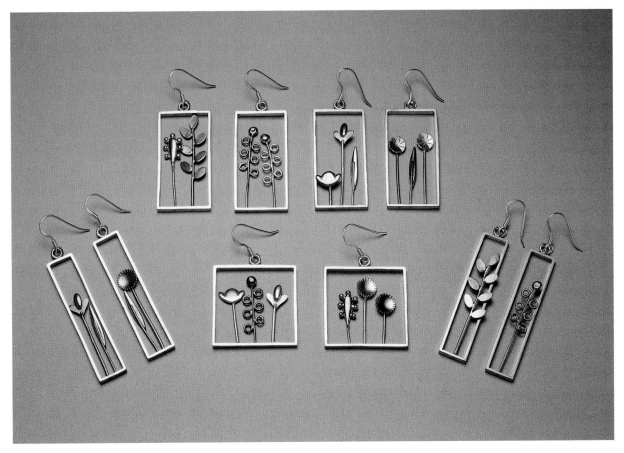

Jae Seung Yoon

The Fresh Life | 2004

1.9 X 4.5 X 0.3 CM (TOP ROW), 1 X 5 X 0.3 CM (BOTTOM, LEFT AND RIGHT), 3 X 3.5 X 0.3 CM (BOTTOM, CENTER)

Sterling silver, brass; hand fabricated

PHOTO BY MYUNG-WOOK HUH

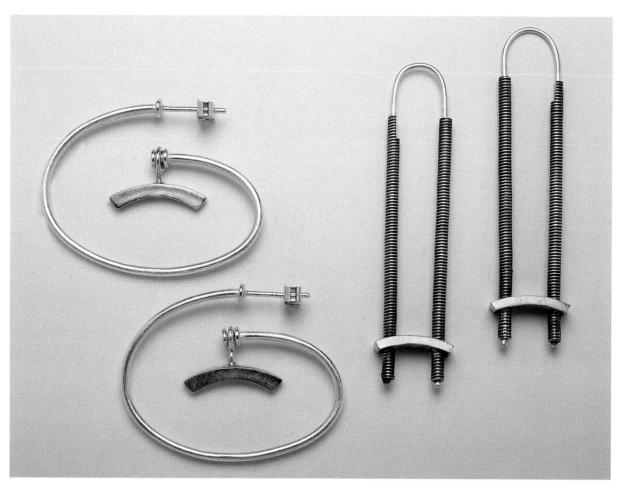

Noon Mitchelhill

Untitled | 2000

LEFT, 3 X 4 CM; RIGHT, 6 X 1 CM

Silver, gold plate; cast,
hand fabricated

PHOTO BY JOËL DEGEN

Derek McKay Duncan
Untitled | 2006
EACH, 7 X 7 X 1 CM
Sterling silver, 18-karat yellow gold,
diamonds; hand fabricated
PHOTOS BY ARTIST

Luana Coonen
Beetle Wing Earrings | 2005
EACH, 5.1 X 5.1 X 0.6 CM
Sterling silver, acrylic, beetle wings;
pierced, riveted
PHOTO BY AMY O'CONNELL

Gina Pankowski
Tighra | 1997–2006
EACH, 3.8 CM TALL
Sterling silver, 14-karat gold, patina
PHOTO BY DOUG YAPLE

Hyejeong Ko

Earrings | 2002

LEFT, 2 X 5 X 1 CM; RIGHT, 2 X 6.5 X 1 CM

Sterling silver; hand fabricated

PHOTOS BY DAN NEUBERGER

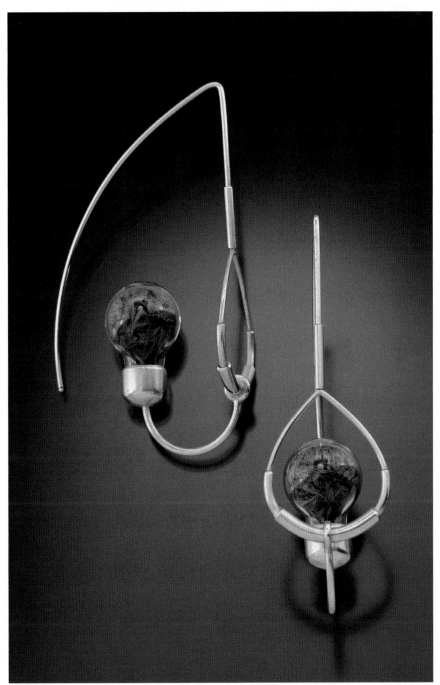

Angela Bubash
Kinetic Earrings | 2005
EACH, 5 X 2.5 X 2.5 CM
Sterling silver, glass, dyed ostrich
feathers; fabricated
PHOTO BY TOM MILLS

Eliana R. Arenas
Naranja | 2006
12.5 X 5 X 5 CM
Sterling silver, handmade
paper; hand fabricated
PHOTO BY MICHAEL O'NEILL

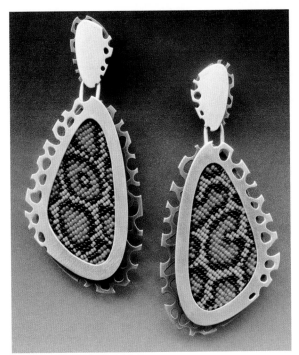

Jessee J. Smith

Burmese Python (Python molurus bivittatus) | 2006
EACH, 6.5 X 2.9 X 0.3 CM
Sterling silver, fine silver, copper, antique 20-percent glass
microbeads, nylon thread; pierced, textured, soldered, loom woven
PHOTO BY RALPH GABRINER

*Much of my work draws upon the ancient Chinese concept
of* li—*the organic, asymmetrical patterns found in nature.*
Li *may be seen in a network of cracks in drying mud, in frost
crystals on a pane of glass, or in the subtly structured spot
patterns of plants and animals. As a biologist, I am endlessly
fascinated by the latter. Literally thousands of varieties of
stripes and spots and rosettes exist, in innumerable
combinations of colors.* JESSEE J. SMITH

Lulu Smith

Coneflower Earring | 2004
EACH, 1.3 X 1 X 0.3 CM
Sterling silver, hand-pigmented
resin; inlay, cast, fabricated
PHOTO BY DOUG YAPLE

*This earring has an empty bezel so that the resin
can glow like glass in the light.* LULU SMITH

Wanjin Kim

Perpetuity | 2006

EACH, 4 X 3 X 0.5 CM

Fine silver, pearls, enamel;
chased, formed

PHOTO BY DAVID TERAO

Giselle Kolb

Earrings | 2005

BOX, 6 X 5 X 2.5 CM; EARRINGS, 5 CM LONG

Sterling silver, fine silver, enamel, freshwater pearls, blue topaz, resin; hand fabricated

PHOTOS BY HAP SAKWA

The earrings are contained in a small shrine (box) so they can be displayed as a small sculpture when not being worn. GISELLE KOLB

Tessa E. Rickard

Deer Talisman | 2006

10.2 X 10.2 X 0.3 CM

Sterling silver, dyed deer fur;
hand fabricated

PHOTO BY TIM CARPENTER

Masako Onodera
Flowers for Daydreaming | 2004
EACH, 5.1 X 2.5 X 2.5 CM
Sterling silver, earplugs;
hand fabricated, oxidized
PHOTO BY ARTIST

Christina Lemon
Ocean Series Earrings | 2005
EACH, 3 X 1.5 X 0.3 CM
Enamel, 14-karat gold,
sterling silver; fabricated
PHOTO BY SETH TICE LEWIS

Annette Ehinger
Unique Pieces | 2006
EACH, 4.2 X 1.4 X 1 CM
14-karat gold, citrine; fabricated,
hand-cut stones, soldered
PHOTO BY ARTIST

Loretta Fontaine

Gravid Series—Etched Sunflower Earrings | 2005

EACH, 3.2 X 2.2 X 1 CM

22-karat gold, 14-karat gold, sterling silver, amethyst,
opal, quartz drozy, freshwater pearls, black and white
photographs, patina; hand fabricated, etched

PHOTO BY ARTIST

Kiwon Wang

Jewel Container | 2003

EACH, 7.6 X 2.5 X 2.5 CM

Sterling silver, newspaper, pearl, 23-karat gold leaf

PHOTO BY JAMES BEARDS

I combine precious and nonprecious materials and create unusual juxtapositions in an attempt to achieve a new kind of harmony in jewelry making and to form a new language I can use to describe my experience an an easterner in a western world.

In the east, the pearl is believed to contain the universe, as it imitates the shape of the earth. The pearl is created from an oyster's suffering, yet has the most incredible, irridescent colors. This paradox is why I was drawn to the pearl. KIWON WANG

Murphy Design, Emily Chesick
Untitled | 2004
EACH, 5 X 1.2 X 1 CM
14-karat gold, abalone mabe pearl,
tanzanite, pink sapphire, diamond
PHOTO BY COREY MORSE

Diana Vincent
Untitled | 2006
EACH, 2.9 X 1.6 CM
18-karat white gold, 18-karat yellow
gold, diamonds, pink tourmaline;
hand fabricated
PHOTO BY ARTIST

Claude Schmitz
Paris II | 2006
EACH, 3 X 2 X 0.8 CM
18-karat gold, pearls;
hand fabricated
PHOTO BY WIM

Marya Dabrowski

Tri-Color Drop Earrings | 2005

EACH, 4 X 1 X 1 CM

18-karat gold, diamond, pink tourmaline,
green tourmaline, amethyst; hand fabricated,
granulation, bezel set

PHOTO BY RALPH GABRINER

Vlad Lavrovsky and Cesar Lim
Blue from *Sogni d'Oro* Collection | 2005
EACH, 10 X 2.5 X 0.5 CM

Blue diamonds, blue zircon, fine silver, 18-karat yellow
gold; cast, hand fabricated, hammered, oxidized
PHOTO BY ARTIST

Grace Wang-Bishop

Pendants | 2003

EACH, 3.2 X 1.3 X 1.9 CM

Sterling silver, simulated
aquamarine; fabricated

PHOTO BY ARTIST

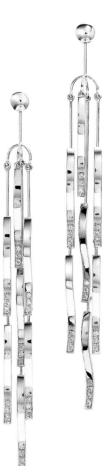

Eddie Sakamoto

Ripples | 2005

EACH, 4 X 0.4 X 0.4 CM

18-karat gold, diamonds;
hand fabricated

PHOTO BY ARTIST

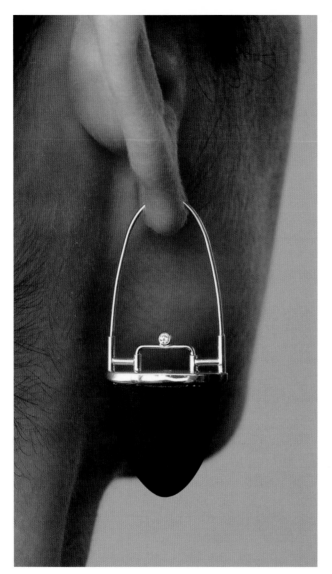

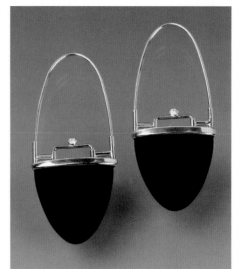

Yas Tanaka

Deco Pendulum Earrings | 2005

EACH, 5.1 X 2.2 X 0.6 CM

18-karat gold, 14-karat gold, frosted
black onyx, diamond; bezel set

PHOTOS BY CHRISTINE DHEIN

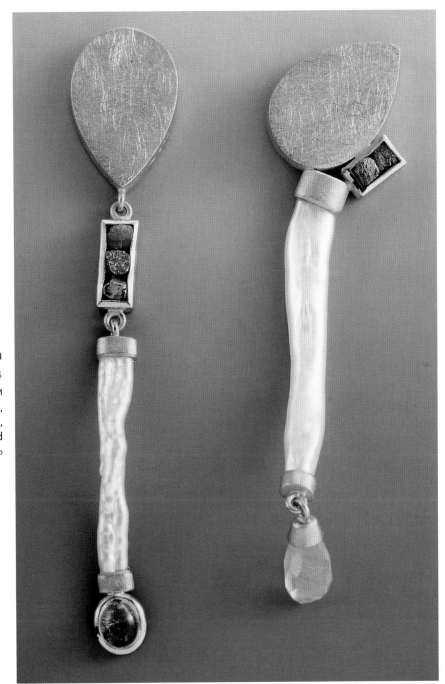

Janis Kerman
Earrings | 2004
EACH, 7 X 2 CM
18-karat yellow gold, pearls,
industrial diamonds, tourmaline,
moonstone; hand fabricated
PHOTO BY DALE GOULD

Beate Klockmann

Apple Earrings | 2006

EACH, 5.5 X 2.5 X 2.5 CM

14-karat gold, enamel,
copper, silver; niello

PHOTO BY ARTIST

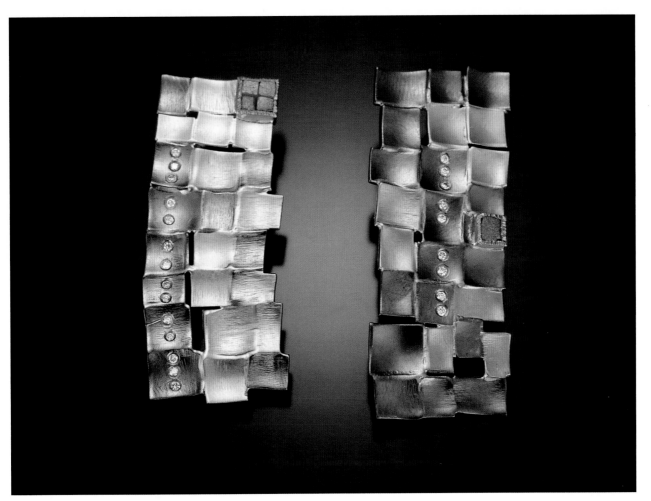

Todd Reed
Untitled | 2005
EACH, 5.5 X 2 X 0.1 CM
18-karat yellow gold, sterling silver,
patina, raw diamonds, cut diamonds;
hand forged, fabricated
PHOTO BY AZAD

Kristine Bolhuis

An Earring Succumbs | 2003

INSTALLATION, 25 X 76 X 18 CM

Steel, 18-karat gold, wood; hand
fabricated with moveable joints

PHOTOS BY JOHN GUILLEMIN

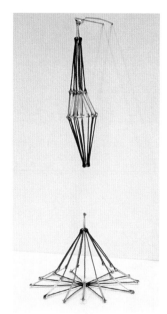

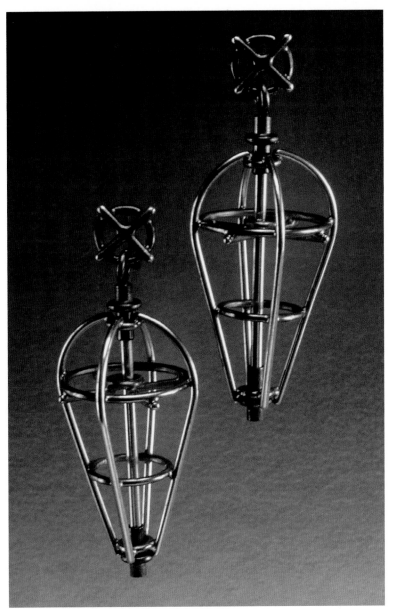

Ben Neubauer

Balloon Earrings | 2004

EACH, 4 X 2 X 2 CM

18-karat gold, sterling silver; hand fabricated, oxidized

PHOTO BY COURTNEY FRISSE

These earrings are based on one of the most traditional forms in jewelry, the teardrop, which I have flipped over to resemble a hot air balloon. BEN NEUBAUER

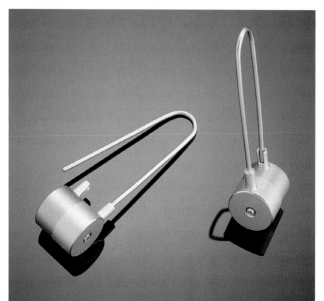

Geoffrey D. Giles
Reversible Tubes | 2005
EACH, 3.2 X 1 X 0.6 CM
18-karat yellow gold, 18-karat white
gold, diamonds; hollow form fabricated,
married metal, brushed finish
PHOTO BY TAYLOR DABNEY

These earrings are half yellow gold, half white gold, and
fully reversible. Either side of the earwire can be put
through the lobe, and once locked in place, the earwire looks
the same from both directions. GEOFFREY D. GILES

Kari Rinn
Elements | 2004
EACH, 6 X 0.5 X 1.5 CM
Steel, 14-karat gold,
diamond; forged
PHOTO BY TAYLOR DABNEY

Daphne Krinos
Untitled | 2004
LARGEST, 6.5 X 1 X 1 CM
Silver, citrine, rock crystal;
hand fabricated, oxidized
PHOTO BY JOËL DEGEN

Christine Dhein

Ear Ornament for a Cyber–Tribal Warrior Princess | 1998

10 X 10.5 X 0.1 CM

Copper, patina; pierced

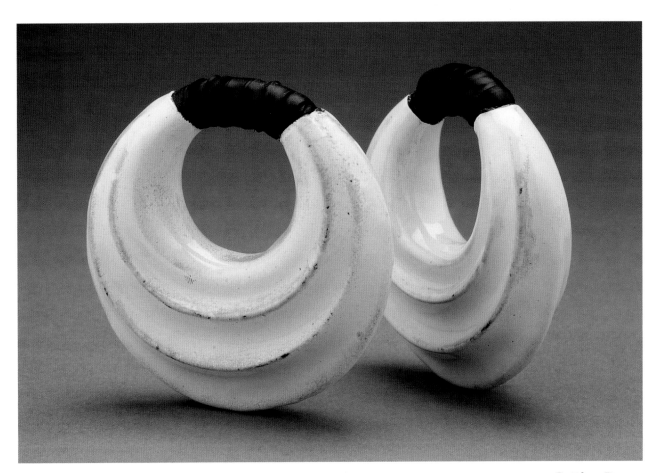

Caitlyn Davey
Untitled | 2004
EACH, 9.5 X 9.5 X 2.5 CM
Recycled rubber, copper,
enamel; 3-D modeled, rapid
prototyped, electroformed
PHOTO BY BILL BACHHUBER

April Higashi
Lava Earrings | 2005
EACH, 6.4 X 1.3 X 0.6 CM
22-karat gold, enamel; underfired
PHOTO BY GEORGE POST

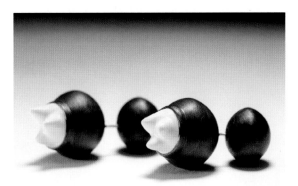

Bridget Catchpole
Curiosities Series | 2006
EACH, 4 X 2 CM
Sterling silver, plastic from found object,
rubber; hand fabricated, oxidized
PHOTOS BY ANTHONY MCLEAN

Barbara Cohen
Cocoon Earrings | 2006
6.5 X 3.5 X 2 CM
Silk cocoons, paint, sterling silver,
cultured pearls; hand fabricated
PHOTO BY ARTIST

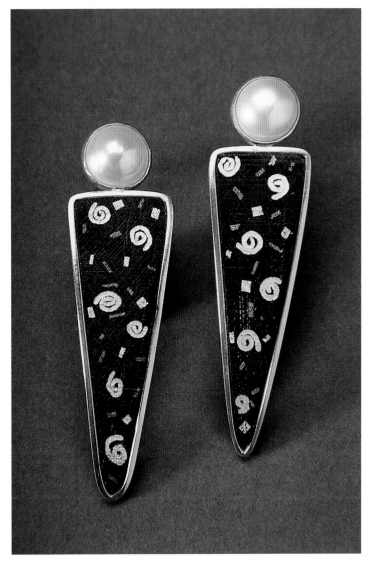

Angela K. Hung

Moonlight II | 2004

EACH, 5.5 X 0.7 X 1.5 CM

24-karat gold, gold leaf, silver leaf, fine silver,
steel, freshwater pearls; hand fabricated,
damascene, oxidized

PHOTO BY ARTIST

57

Christa Lühtje
Untitled | 1998
EACH, 2.3 X 2.3 X 0.3 CM
22-karat gold, onyx; cut, set
PHOTO BY PHILIPP SCHÖNBORN

Mijin Bark
Other Voices | 2006
6.5 X 8.5 X 2.5 CM
Sterling silver, copper,
gold leaf; electroformed
PHOTO BY MYUNG-WOOK HUH, STUDIO MUNCH

Dennis Nahabetian

Stellar Earrings | 2004

3 X 3 X 1.5 CM

Bronze, copper, 14-karat gold, 24-karat
gold plate; electroformed, fabricated

PHOTO BY ARTIST; MODEL, DIANA RUPP

Cathy Chotard
Untitled | 2006
EACH, 4.2 X 0.8 X 0.3 CM
18-karat gold, nylon thread
PHOTO BY ARTIST

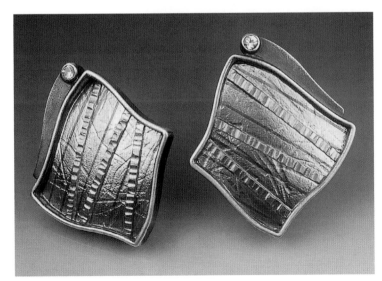

Birgit Kupke-Peyla
Untitled | 2005
EACH, 3.4 X 3.4 X 0.4 CM
22-karat gold, sterling silver, white
sapphire; hand fabricated, roller printed,
hammered, intarsia inlay, oxidized
PHOTO BY DAVID DRUEDING

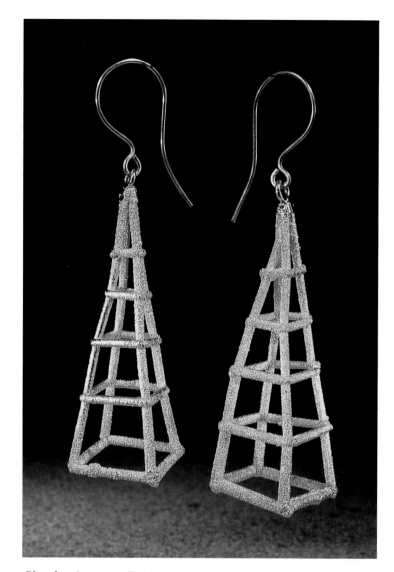

Charles Lewton-Brain
Earrings B299 | 2004
EACH, 5.7 X 2 CM
Stainless steel, copper, 24-karat
gold; fusion welded, electroformed
PHOTO BY ARTIST

Jacqueline Ryan
Untitled | 2000
EACH, 2.6 X 2.6 X 0.9 CM
18-karat gold; hand fabricated
PHOTO BY GIOVANNI CORVAJA
COURTESY OF CHARON KRANSEN ARTS,
NEW YORK, NEW YORK

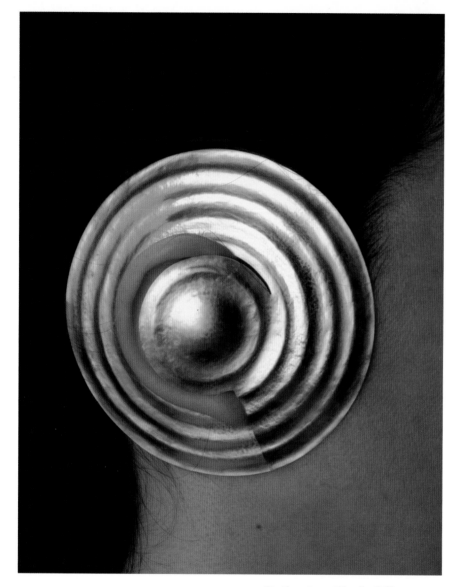

Catherine Clark Gilbertson
Earpiece #1 | 2003
2.6 X 8.6 CM
18-karat gold; chased, repoussé

PHOTOS BY JIM WILDEMAN

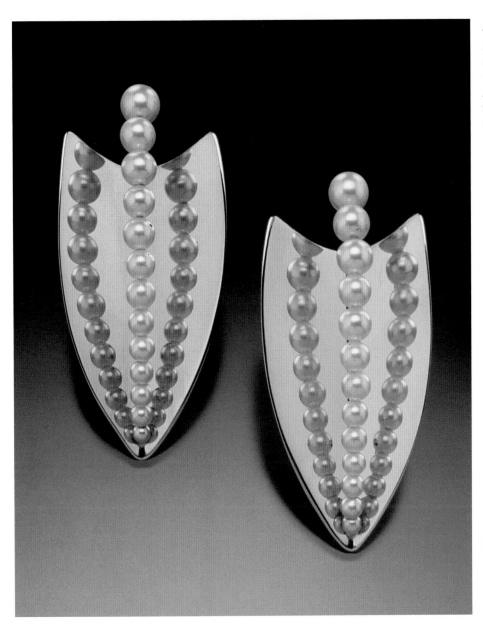

Alan Revere

Pearl Reflections | 1992

EACH, 4 X 2 X 1.6 CM

18-karat gold, platinum,
Akoya cultured pearls;
formed, fabricated

PHOTO BY BARRY BLAU

*Experimenting with
reflections, I discovered
how to make pearls multiply.*

ALAN REVERE

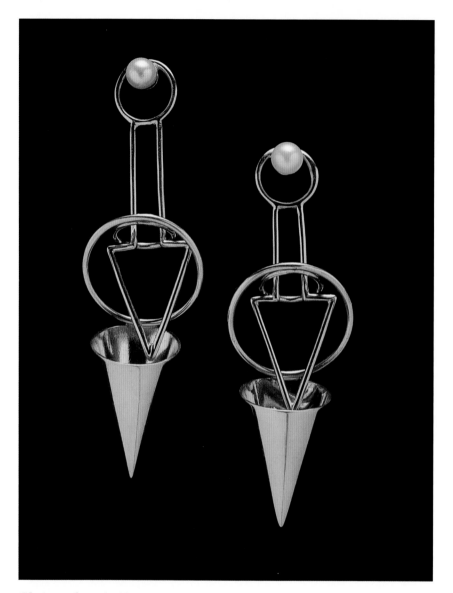

Christopher A. Hentz

Arrows and Cones | 1999

EACH, 3.1 X 1.6 X 1.6 CM

14-karat yellow gold, pearls; fabricated

PHOTO BY RALPH GABRINER

Charles Lewton-Brain
Untitled | 2001
EACH, 4 X 2.5 CM
18-karat gold; fold formed, forged
PHOTO BY ARTIST

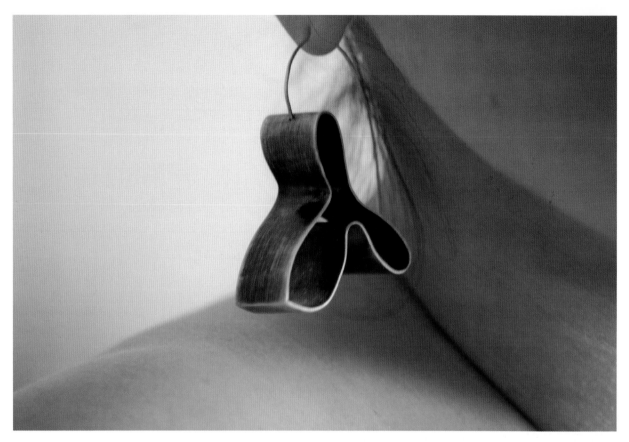

Claudia Costa

Untitled | 2006

EACH, 4.5 X 3.5 X 1.4 CM

22-karat gold, silver; oxidized

PHOTOS BY STEFANO VIGNI

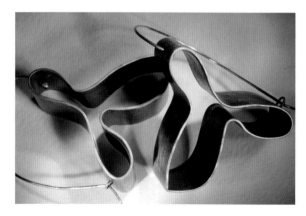

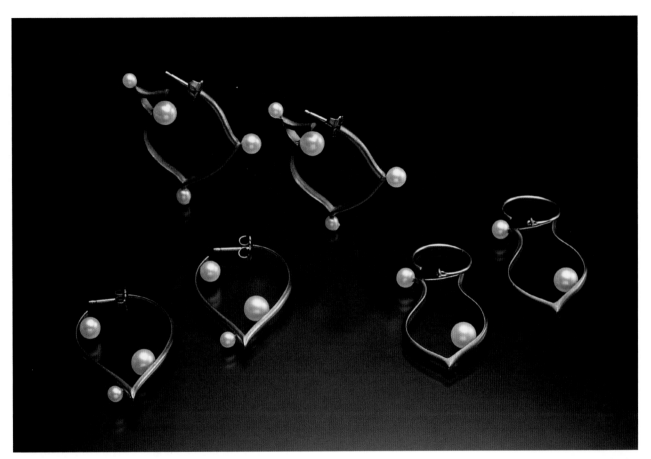

Mark Kanazawa
Untitled | 2005
LARGEST, 3 X 3.5 X 0.3 CM
Sterling silver, freshwater
cultured pearls; fabricated,
cast, oxidized
PHOTO BY GUY NICOL

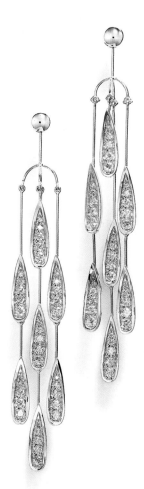

Eddie Sakamoto

Bubbles | 2005

EACH, 2.7 X 1.1 X 0.3 CM

18-karat gold, diamonds;
cast, hand fabricated

PHOTO BY ARTIST

Diana Vincent
Untitled | 2006
EACH, 1.8 X 2 CM
18-karat white gold, silver, diamonds;
hand fabricated, oxidized
PHOTO BY ARTIST

Patricia Tschetter
Untitled | 2005
EACH, 2.2 X 2.2 X 0.9 CM
22-karat gold, 18-karat gold, sapphires, peridot; hand fabricated, granulation
PHOTO BY ROBERT DIAMANTE

The addition of a hook on the back allows the wearer many options. Here, they are shown with the peridot briolette drops, which can be removed. PATRICIA TSCHETTER

Mattioli

Mattioli Hiroko Earrings | 2005

EACH, 2 X 5.5 CM

18-karat yellow gold, natural horn, 18-karat white gold, diamonds, mother-of-pearl

PHOTO BY ARTIST

Abrasha

Untitled | 1993

EACH, 3.8 X 1 CM

18-karat gold, stainless steel, hematite; hand fabricated

PHOTO BY ARTIST

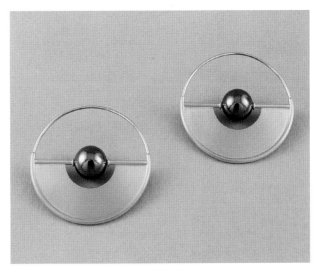

Janice Grzyb
King and Queen | 2005
EACH, 6.4 X 1.9 X 0.6 CM
22-karat gold, 18-karat gold,
precious and semi-precious
stones, pearl; hand fabricated
PHOTO BY RALPH GABRINER

Claire Bersani
Sapphire Crystal Earrings | 2003
EACH, 6.5 X 1.5 CM
Sapphire crystals, cultured
pearls, 22-karat gold
PHOTO BY STEFAN HAGEN

Tami Dean

Glitz Kick Earrings | 2006

EACH, 5 X 1.3 X 0.3 CM

18-karat gold, 14-karat gold, mild steel,
rainbow pyrite, spinel, diamonds; hand
forged, fabricated, cast, soldered, oxidized

PHOTO BY HAP SAKWA

Deborrah Daher

Red, White, and Blue Earrings | 2002

EACH, 3.8 X 1.3 X 0.5 CM

22-karat gold, 18-karat gold, lapis lazuli,
garnet, pearl; hand fabricated

PHOTO BY ARTIST

Shihoko Amano
Nazuna #3 | 2003
EACH, 5 X 2 X 2 CM
18-karat gold, boxwood,
dye; fabricated
PHOTO BY ARTIST

Marjorie Schick
Night Bloom | 2003

EACH EARRING, 4 X 5.3 X 0.5 CM; ON
STAND, 37.5 X 34.9 X 4.4 CM

Wood, plastic laminate, paint,
stainless steel ear posts; constructed

PHOTOS BY GARY POLLMILLER

Julia M. Barello
Small Flowers | 2005

8 X 3.5 CM

Dyed x-ray film, monofilament;
hand fabricated, heat treated

PHOTO BY MICHAEL O'NEILL

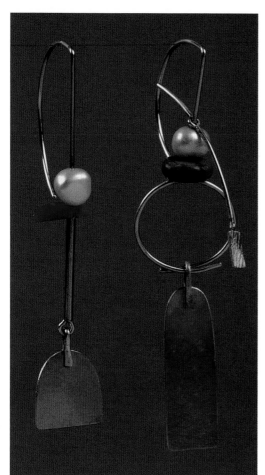

Micki Lippe
Now and Then | 2006
EACH, 5.5 X 2 X 0.5 CM
22-karat gold, sterling silver, pearls, turquoise, coral; hand fabricated
PHOTO BY RICHARD NICOL

Where is it written that earrings should match? MICKI LIPPE

John Cogswell
Homage to Charles | 2005
EACH, 5 X 2.3 CM
Sterling silver, blue chalcedony;
fold formed, fabricated
PHOTO BY ARTIST

I love to eat chocolate. As a child, I especially loved to eat a
sweet called "chocolate beetles." People recognize the origin of
these earring forms and ask me about them and tell me their favorite
childhood eating customs. BEATE EISMANN

Beate Eismann
Chocolate Beetles | 2006
LARGEST, 7 X 4.7 X 1.2 CM
Aluminum, steel wire;
sawed, anodized
PHOTO BY ARTIST

Anna Kukuchek

Pin Earrings | 2006

EACH, 6.8 X 3.5 X 3.5 CM

Sterling silver, polycarbonate,
sewing pins; hand fabricated

PHOTO BY MIRANDA WALL

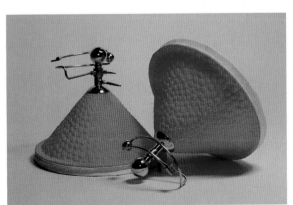

Mi-Mi Moscow
Eye of Ear | 2003
EACH, 8.4 X 0.9 X 7 CM
Nickel silver, paper, pigment

Annamaria Zanella

Black | 2005

EACH, 3.5 X 2 X 1.5 CM

Silver, patina, glass, gold;
hand fabricated

PHOTO BY GIULIO RUSTICHELLI

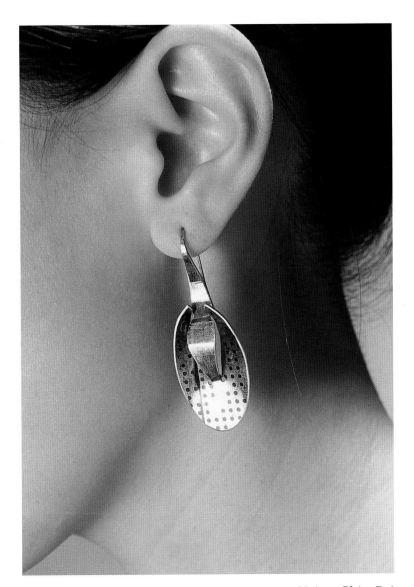

Hsiao Chia-Pei
Change | 2005
EACH, 5 X 2.5 X 1 CM
Aluminum, dye; anodized
PHOTOS BY ARTIST

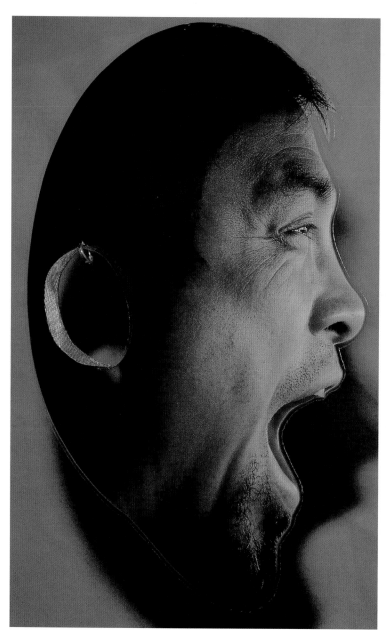

Hsueh-Ying Wu

Listening | 2006

26 X 17 X 0.3 CM

Stainless mesh, sterling silver,
photograph; hand fabricated

PHOTOS BY CHIN-TING CHIU

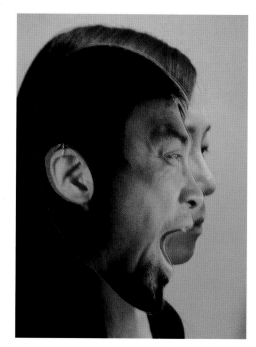

Rebecca Hannon
Trefoil Earrings | 2005
EACH, 9 X 3 X 0.3 CM
Compact discs, silver; cut,
shaped, set, hand fabricated
PHOTO BY ARTIST

Hannah Louise Lamb
Oval Curve Leaf Mismatch Earrings | 2006
LEFT, 4.5 X 2.5 X 0.1 CM
Silver; hand pierced, oxidized
PHOTO BY ARTIST

The kiwi, cut from a New Zealand dollar, is set in a cage on a shamrock. The kiwi cut from a U.S. coin is free to roam. This work reflects the inevitable situation that the American dollar affects the strength of the New Zealand dollar. PETER DECKERS

Peter Deckers
Inclusion (detained by freedom), earclip and earring | 2002
LARGEST, 6.2 X 3.5 X 3.5 CM
Sterling silver, currency from New Zealand and the United States; cut, fabricated
PHOTO BY ARTIST

Karen Bachmann
Spear Ears | 2005
EACH, 7.5 X 1 X 1 CM
Ebony, thermoplastic acrylic resin,
sterling silver; laminated, hand
carved, polished, sandblasted
PHOTO BY KRONUS PHOTO

Satomi Kawai

Cultural Transformation Device: Negative Gradation | 2006

7 X 22 X 10 CM

Copper, silver, brass, acrylic rod, paint, nuts, bolts, fabric; hand fabricated, riveted

PHOTOS BY CHIEKO ARAI

Jan Wehrens
Earrings | 2006
EACH, 7 X 5.6 X 1.6 CM
Steel, vinyl
PHOTO BY ANGELA BRÖHAN

Daphne Krinos
Untitled | 2005
EACH, 5.8 X 2.2 X 0.3 CM
Silver, rutilated quartz; hand
fabricated, oxidized
PHOTO BY JOËL DEGEN

Johan Van Aswegen
Tear Drops

Enamel, sterling silver,
fine gold; oxidized
PHOTO BY ARTIST

Eileen Gerstein
Untitled | 1999
EACH, 2.5 X 3 X 0.5 CM

22-karat gold bimetal, sterling silver, 24-karat gold, patina; hand fabricated, riveted, kum boo

PHOTO BY ARTIST

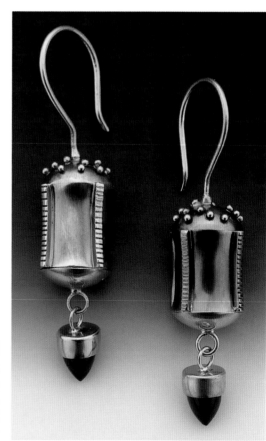

Kathy Kovel
Lantern Earrings | 2006
EACH, 5 X 1.2 X 1.2 CM
Sterling silver, 18-karat yellow gold, garnet; oxidized
PHOTO BY GEORGE POST

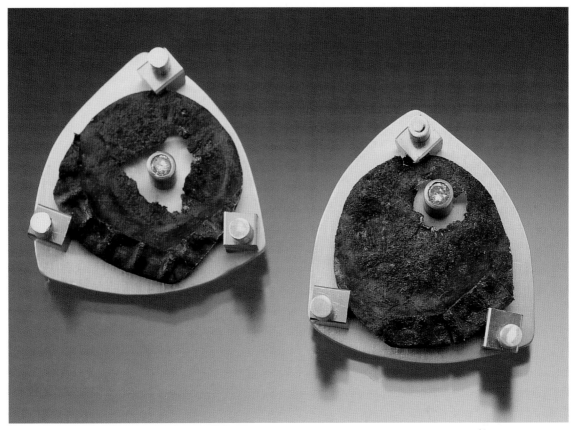

Shannon Cobb-Tappan

Untitled | 2006

EACH, 3 X 3 X 1.8 CM

Sterling silver, 18-karat yellow gold, diamond,
found bottle caps; hand fabricated

PHOTOS BY TOM MCCARTHY

Polly Daeger
Untitled | 2005
EACH, 7 X 1.5 X 1.5 CM
Copper; fold formed, cut, coiled
PHOTO BY LARRY SANDERS

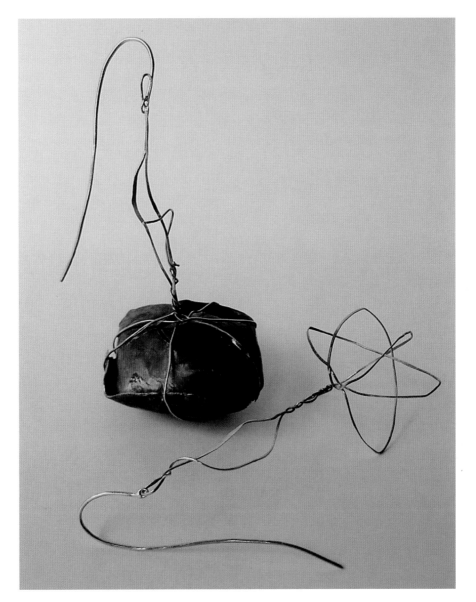

Noriko Hanawa

Present from Forest | 2005

LEFT, 9 X 4 X 3 CM; RIGHT, 8 X 4 X 3 CM

18-karat gold, shibuishi; hand fabricated

PHOTO BY ARTIST

Helen Ellison-Dorion

Untitled | 2003

EACH, 9.5 X 2.5 X 2.5 CM

Sterling silver, fine silver, enamel,
patina; hand fabricated

PHOTO BY ARTIST

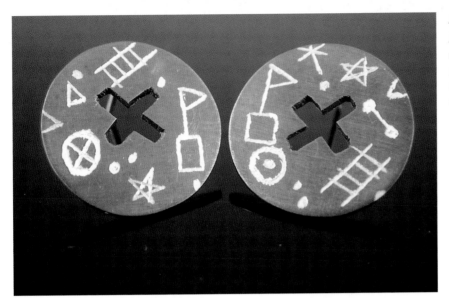

Alexis Romeo
Symbol Earrings | 2005
EACH, 2 X 2 X 0.1 CM
Sterling silver, patina;
hand fabricated
PHOTO BY PAUL ROMEO

Ingeborg Vandamme
Cone Earrings | 1998
EACH, 6.5 X 3.5 X 1.5 CM
Copper, paraffined paper
PHOTO BY ARTIST

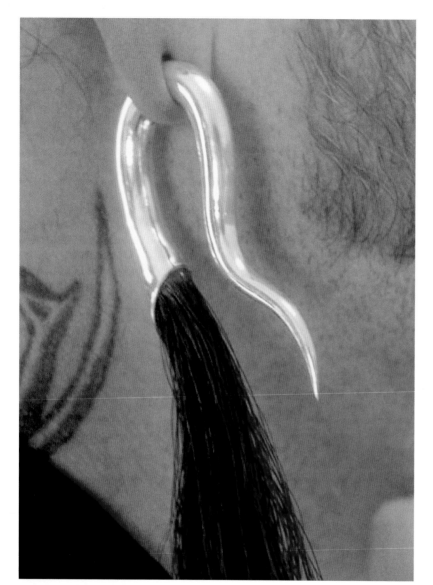

Kelly A. Orbanic

Horse Hair Earrings | 2004

EACH, 27 X 1 X 3 CM

Sterling silver, horse hair;
forged, fabricated

PHOTOS BY JENNIFER G. WALL

Gretchen Walker
Untitled | 2006
EACH, 3.5 X 5.4 X 3.5 CM
Copper; anticlastic raising
PHOTO BY SHADI YOUSEFIAN

Maureen Brusa Zappellini

Root System | 2006

EACH, 3 X 2 X 0.5 CM

Mixed metals, silver, copper; hollow constructed, fabricated, hammered

PHOTO BY ROBIN STANCLIFF
COURTESY OF OBSIDIAN GALLERY, TUCSON, ARIZONA

I like to keep my earrings wearable and intimate. I try to engineer some movement interest in these pieces, making the viewer want to come in closer to look—perhaps as a prelude to a kiss? MAUREEN BRUSA ZAPPELLINI

Jun Park

Eye Cannot Tell a Lie | 2006

EACH, 3.3 X 2.3 X 0.5 CM

Sterling silver, nickel, toy eye;
hand fabricated, heat colored

PHOTOS BY MYUNG-WOOK HUH

Laurie Dansereau
Fertile Alveolus | 2006
EACH, 9 X 3 X 3 CM
Sterling silver, violet wood, garnets;
hand fabricated, sculpted, oxidized
PHOTO BY ANTHONY MCLEAN

Yuyen Chang
Untitled | 2006
EACH, 1.5 X 1.5 X 0.3 CM
18-karat gold and silver
bimetal; repoussé
PHOTO BY TOM MCINVALLE

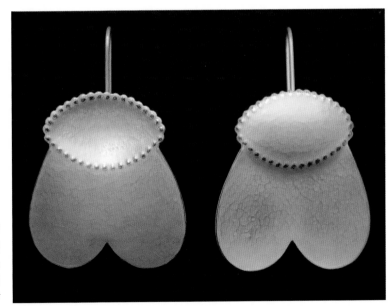

Birgit Laken
Heartwear Earrings | 2006
EACH, 4.5 X 4 X 0.4 CM
Silver; pressed, chased
PHOTO BY ARTIST

Nisa Smiley
White Herons | 2002
EACH, 6.4 X 1.9 X 0.2 CM
Sterling silver; pierced, hand
fabricated, oxidized
PHOTO BY ROBERT DIAMANTE

Keri Ataumbi
Bugs on Hoops | 2006
EACH, 5 X 5 X 0.5 CM
Silver; hand fabricated, oxidized
PHOTO BY JAMES HART

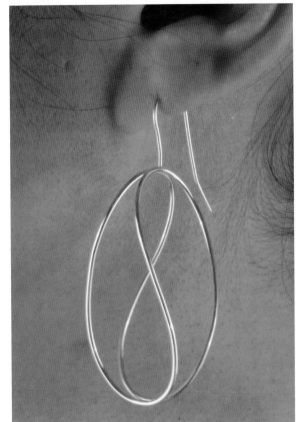

Sun Kyoung Kim
Link | 2006
5.1 X 2.5 X 2.5 CM
Sterling silver
PHOTO BY ARTIST

Lori Meg Gottlieb
Lattice Earrings | 2006
EACH, 5 X 1 X 0.3 CM
Sterling silver; cast, fabricated
PHOTO BY JOSEPH HYDE

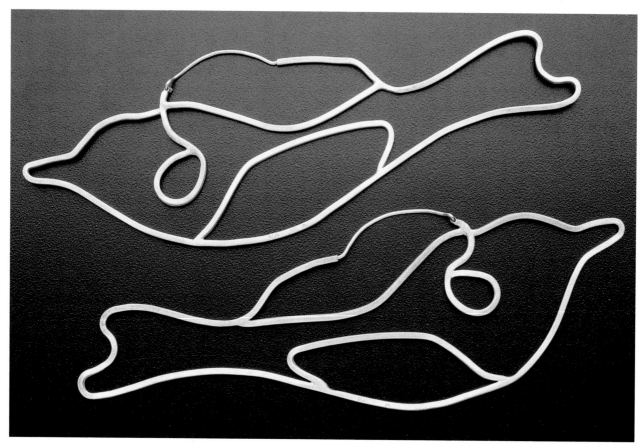

Keri Ataumbi
Bird Hoops | 2006
EACH, 5.5 X 16 X 0.1 CM
Sterling silver; hand fabricated
PHOTO BY JOEL MULLER

Maarten Van Der Vegte
Labels | 2006
EACH, 2.8 X 1.8 X 0.1 CM
Sterling silver, silk thread
PHOTOS BY ARTIST

Jonathan Hernandez

From the series *Interstellar Bldg. Suite* | 2006

EACH, 13 X 10 CM

Brass

PHOTO BY ROBLY GLOVER

Cuyler Hovey-King
Bird Cage Earrings | 2006
EACH, 7.9 X 2.2 X 2.2 CM
14-karat yellow gold, sterling silver;
wax carved, cast, fabricated
PHOTOS BY ARTIST

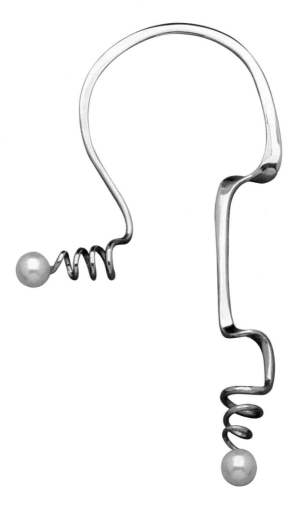

Jim Cohen

Earpiece for the Millenium | 2002

5.5 X 3.5 X 0.5 CM

18-karat gold, pearls; forged

PHOTO BY JIM WILDEMAN

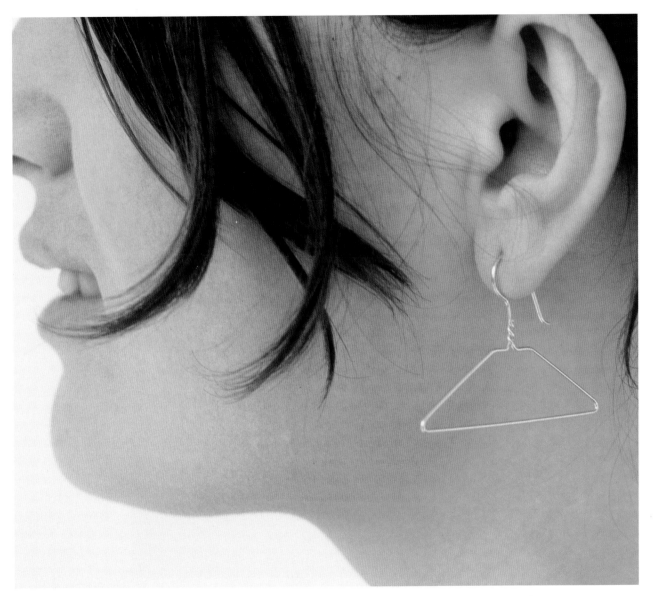

Jiro Kamata
Gold Hanger | 2002
2.5 X 4 X 0.1 CM
18-karat gold
PHOTO BY ARTIST

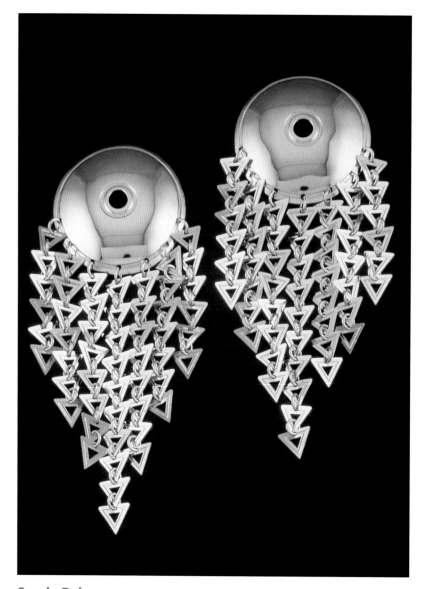

Sandy Baker

Mambo | 1995

EACH, 9.8 X 3.5 X 0.2 CM

18-karat gold; photoetched,
hand fabricated

PHOTO BY ARTIST

Jeanine Payer

Delphine | 2005

EACH, 5.1 X 2.2 X 1.9 CM

18-karat gold, diamond; wax carved, cast, hand engraved

PHOTO BY RONNIE TSAI

Sarah Penny

Untitled | 2005

EACH, 7 X 2 X 1.5 CM

Sterling silver, 18-karat yellow gold; hand fabricated, fold formed, depletion gilded

PHOTO BY ARTIST

Lina Peterson
Hollow Bead Earrings | 2005
EACH, 11 X 6 X 1.5 CM
Plastic, silver, cotton thread
PHOTO BY AMANDA MANSELL

By engaging with both the aesthetic and associative qualities of materials, my making process is one of intuitive decisions about scale, form, and color. I have an experimental approach and a developed confidence in working with a range of materials. Depending on the ideas driving it, my work incorporates materials such as rubber, metals, ceramics, and textiles. LINA PETERSON

Hu Jun
Untitled | 2006
EACH, 15 X 11 X 11 CM
Paper, brass; hand fabricated
PHOTO BY ARTIST

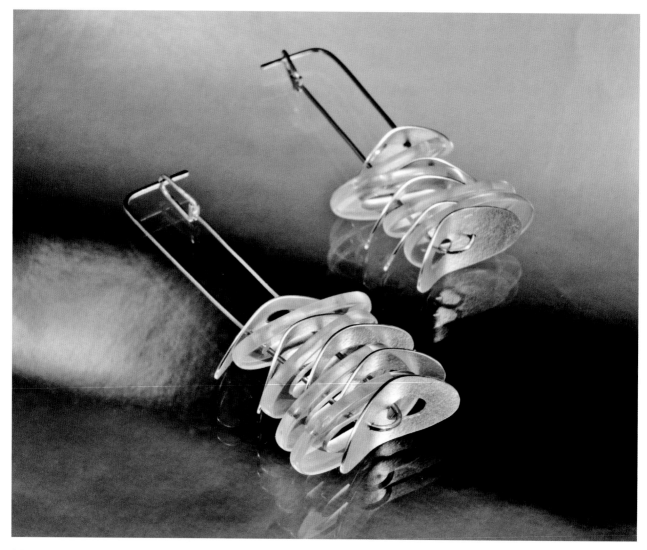

Maria Constanza Ochoa V.
Kiwi | 2005
EACH, 15 X 2.3 X 1.1 CM
Sterling silver, thermoplastic;
hand fabricated
PHOTO BY EMILIANO MOSCOSO

Eliana R. Arenas
Azvoar | 2006
12.5 X 7 X 7 CM
Sterling silver, handmade
paper; hand fabricated
PHOTO BY MICHAEL O'NEILL

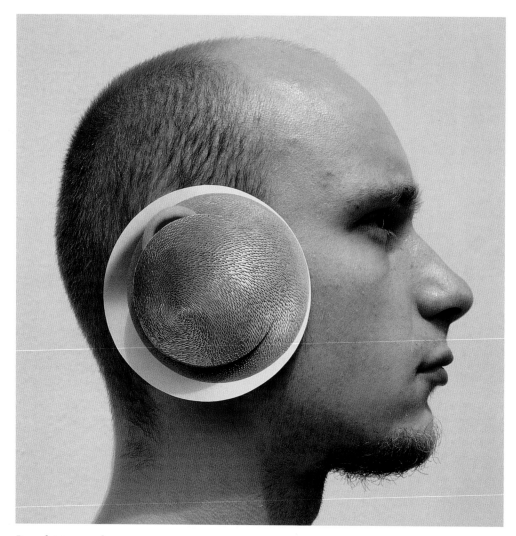

Pavel Herynek
Ear Ornament | 2002
(from the *Ear Ornaments* series, 2002–2006)
10 CM IN DIAMETER
Cardboard, postcard; cut
PHOTO BY ARTIST

Beate Eismann
Anagrammage—28 Earring Sets | 2005
SCREEN: 21 X 31 X 0.8 CM
Copper, enamel, sterling silver
PHOTO BY ARTIST

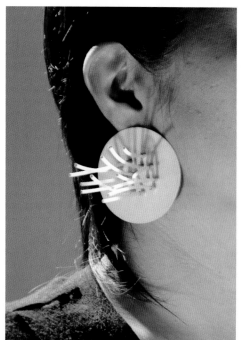

Satomi Kawai
Visual Cue I: Sea Anemone | 2006
7 X 6 X 6 CM
Fine silver, ABS plastic, gold leaf;
hand fabricated
PHOTO BY CHIEKO ARAI

Leonor Hipólito
Object for Dreams 1 | 2004
EACH, 21 X 1.7 X 1.4 CM
Silver, river pearls, silk thread
PHOTO BY ARTIST

Objects for Dreamers *is a series of ear objects. This group of jewels symbolizes moments of introspection, the rise of the inner reality to the surface of one's consciousness. The direct connection between their shapes and the common head-phone suggests isolation and the building of an imaginary world.* LEONOR HIPÓLITO

Kathleen R. Prindiville
Petri | 2006
EACH, 7.3 X 5.6 X 0.5 CM
Sterling silver, thermoplastic;
hand fabricated, carved
PHOTO BY MARTY DOYLE PHOTOGRAPHY

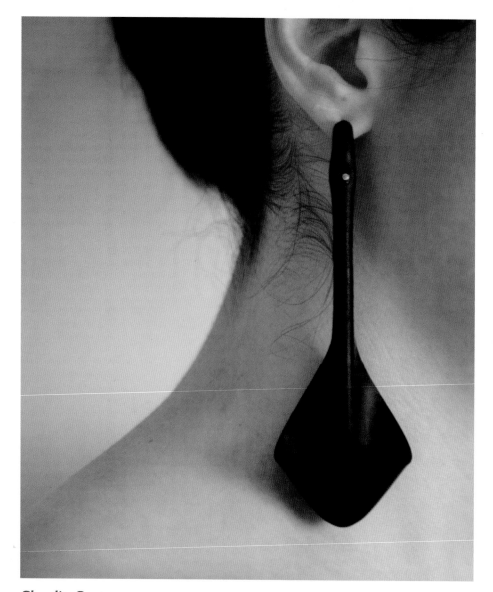

Claudia Costa
Rubbery | 2006
11.5 X 4 X 2.5 CM
Silver, rubber
PHOTO BY STEFANO VIGNI

Anna Lorich

Landscape Earrings | 2006

EACH, 5.1 X 1.9 X 1.3 CM

Plastic, resin, photograph,
14-karat gold

PHOTO BY KATIA KULENKAMPFT

Charmaine Ho

The Witching Hour | 2006

EACH, 7 X 4 X 1.8 CM

Sterling silver, lace; hand
fabricated, sewn

PHOTO BY GEORGE POST

Johan Van Aswegen

Basket Earrings

Fine gold, diamonds,
enamel; formed

PHOTO BY ARTIST

Masumi Kataoka
Memento 2 | 2006
LARGEST, 18 X 13 X 2 CM
18-karat gold, 18-karat bimetal,
sterling silver, steel, copper, enamel,
animal intestine; hand fabricated,
chased, repoussé
PHOTOS BY ARTIST AND GARLAND FIELDER

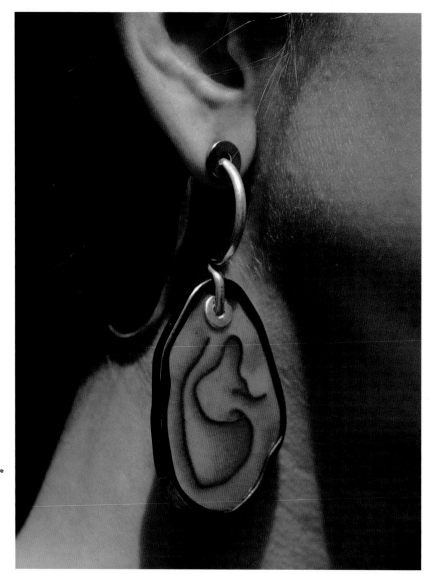

jessica foster
Do Your Ears Hang Low? | 2006
8 X 3.5 X 5 CM
Enamel, copper, sterling silver,
patina; layered, fabricated
PHOTO BY ARTIST

Leonor Hipólito
Object for Dreams 2 | 2006
69.5 X 1.7 X 1.2 CM
Polyester with pigment, silk thread
PHOTO BY ARTIST

Laurie Boisvert
Retractable Rapunzel | 2006
4 X 3 X 2.5 CM
Silver, pine; fabricated
PHOTO BY ARTIST

129

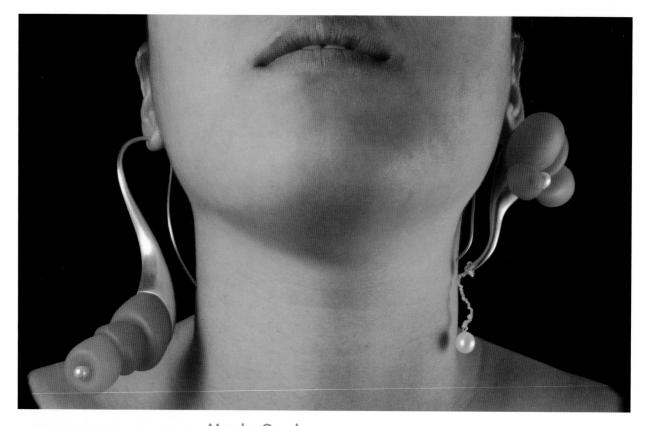

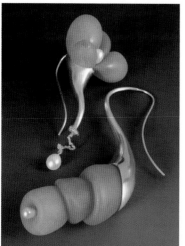

Masako Onodera

The Mating Season | 2006

9.5 X 4.5 X 4 CM AND 11.5 X 2.6 X 6 CM

Sterling silver, freshwater pearls, polyethylene cord, rubber; formed, fabricated, dyed

PHOTOS BY ARTIST

Stephanie White

Hanging Roses | 2006

EACH, 3.5 X 1.5 X 1 CM

Borosilicate glass; lampworked

PHOTO BY ARTIST
COURTESY OF BEADS BY DESIGN, MARIETTA, GEORGIA

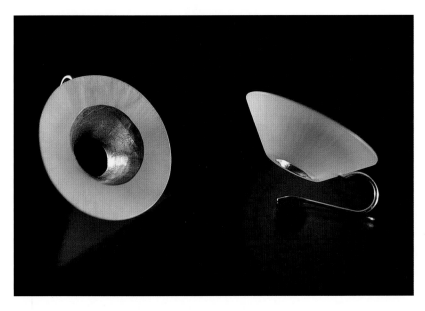

Karen McCreary

Cone Drop Earrings | 1998

EACH, 3 X 3 X 1 CM

Acrylic, 22-karat gold leaf, sterling silver; hand fabricated, carved

PHOTO BY ARTIST

Michelle Nowlan
Diamondback | 2006
EACH, 5.4 X 4 X 0.4 CM
Sterling silver, pyrite;
hand fabricated
PHOTO BY ARTIST

Debbie Jackson
Eggshell Mosaic Earrings | 2006
EACH, 5.1 X 1.9 CM
Polymer clay, dyed eggshells, liquid
polymer clay, grout tinted with mica
powder, freshwater pearls, niobium wire
PHOTO BY KOJO KAMAU

I have always loved mosaics, and I enjoy dying
eggshells and embedding them, one fragment at a
time, into polymer clay. The "vertebrae" half-disks and
tinted grout pull the composition together. DEBBIE JACKSON

Shu-Lin Wu
Reproduction | 2002
14.5 X 5 X 1.5 CM
Silver, resin
PHOTO BY ARTIST

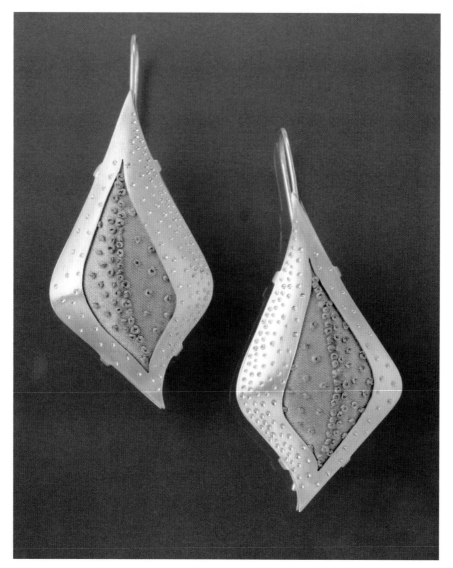

Chelsea E. Bird

Forbidden Knots | 2006

EACH, 6.5 X 2.7 X 1.3 CM

Argentium sterling silver, silk satin,
silk thread; hydraulic pressed, drilled,
soldered, embroidered

PHOTO BY ARTIST

Dianne Karg Baron
Spring Has Sprung, the Grass Is Riz | 2006
5.3 X 3.1 X 3.5 CM
Sterling silver, grass, nylon stocking,
thread; hand forged, bent
PHOTOS BY ARTIST

Annette Ehinger
Unique Pieces | 2005
EACH, 2.8 X 0.8 X 0.8 CM
14-karat gold, amethyst; fabricated,
hand-cut stones, soldered
PHOTO BY ARTIST

Besides jewelry, I'm very interested in other fields of art, such as music, theater, and painting. This is reflected in my work, which often has a playful lightness and shows the pleasure of improvisation. ANNETTE EHINGER

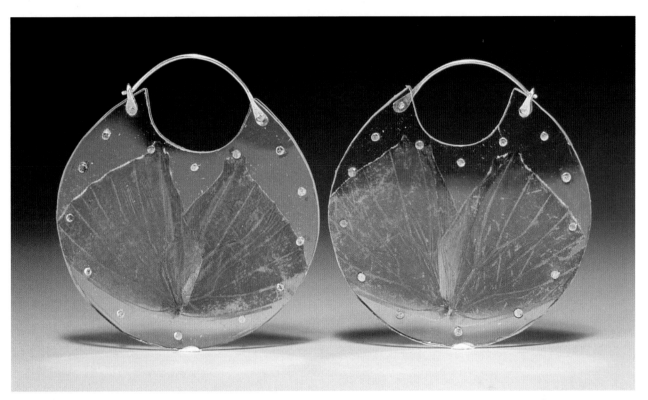

Luana Coonen
Morpho Encasements | 2005
EACH, 5.1 X 5.1 X 0.6 CM
Sterling silver, acrylic, butterfly
wings; cut, riveted, forged
PHOTO BY AMY O'CONNELL

Marya Dabrowski

Fireworks Earrings | 2005

EACH, 3 X 2 X 1 CM

18-karat gold, amethyst, pink tourmaline,
peridot, apatite, tanzanite; hand fabricated,
granulation, wire wrapped

PHOTO BY RALPH GABRINER
COLLECTION OF THE GEMOLOGICAL INSTITUTE
OF AMERICA MUSEUM, CARLSBAD, CALIFORNIA

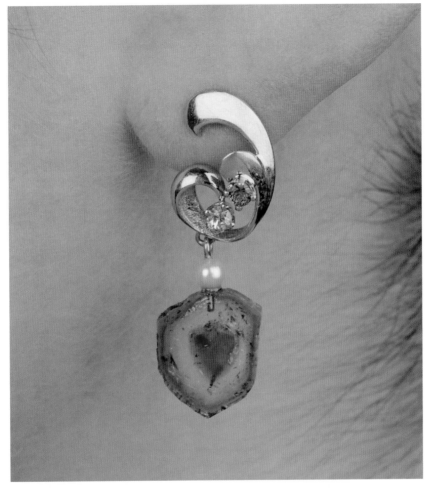

Jo-Ann Maggiora Donivan

Springtime in San Francisco | 2006

EACH, 3.8 X 1.2 X 0.6 CM

14-karat yellow gold, pearls, tourmaline,
22-karat gold; cast, hand textured, overlay

PHOTOS BY ARTIST

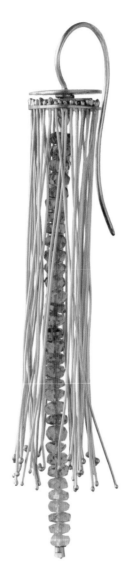

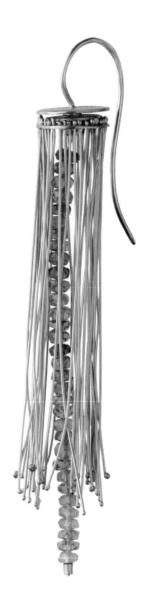

Marcus Teipel

Lluvia | 2005

EACH, 6.5 X 1 X 1 CM

18-karat gold, 22-karat gold, tourmaline

PHOTO BY JUAN VENTURA
COURTESY OF WWW.KLIMT02.NET, BARCELONA, SPAIN

Cecelia Bauer

Fan Earrings | 2001

EACH, 4.9 X 2.9 X 0.6 CM

22-karat gold, amethyst, diamond, seed pearls,
chrysoprase; granulation, repoussé, hand fabricated

PHOTO BY ED ADDEO

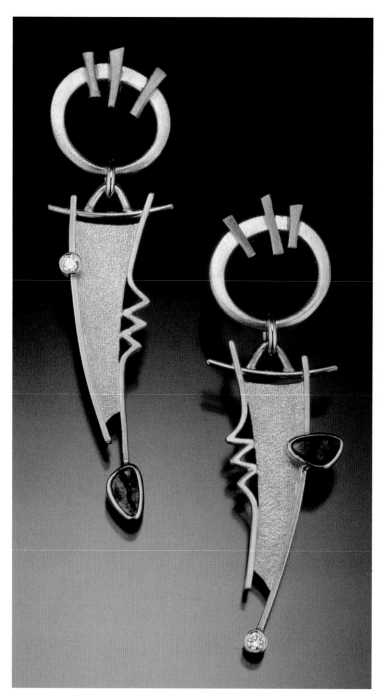

Tami Dean
Quirky Girls | 1998
EACH, 4.5 X 1.8 X 2.8 CM
14-karat palladium white gold, 18-karat gold,
opals, diamonds; hand forged, fabricated
PHOTO BY HAP SAKWA

*My earrings reflect my passion for
well-crafted minutiae, and I love the
challenge of designing pieces that will be
viewed from all directions. They should be
as interesting and nicely finished on the
back as on the front.* TAMI DEAN

Tracy Johnson
Untitled | 2005
EACH, 3.5 X 2 X 0.8 CM
18-karat gold, 22-karat gold, aquamarine, pink sapphire; hand fabricated, bezel set, hinged
PHOTO BY ROBERT DIAMANTE

Kathy Kovel
Camera Lens Earrings | 2006
EACH, 4.5 X 1 X 1.2 CM
18-karat yellow gold, sterling silver, camera lens, metallic pink thread; hand fabricated
PHOTO BY GEORGE POST

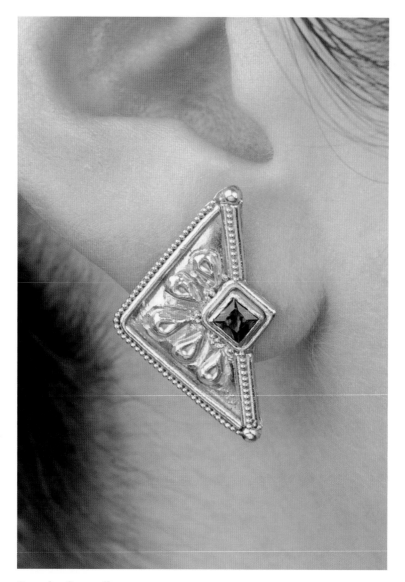

Ronda Coryell
Untitled | 2006
EACH, 3 X 1.8 CM

22-karat gold, blue sapphires;
chased, repoussé, granulation

PHOTO BY CHRISTINE DHEIN

Beth Rosengard

Neon Dusters | 2005

EACH, 4.7 X 1.4 X 0.5 CM

14-karat gold, 18-karat gold,
22-karat gold, apatite, boulder opals;
hand fabricated, broom cast

PHOTO BY ARTIST

In broom casting, molten metal is
poured over the soaking wet, upturned
bristles of a straw broom. The results vary
greatly, but generally echo the dripping,
columnar shapes of stalactites. While
some of these one-of-a-kind castings are
usable in their raw state, I modify, refine,
and combine most of them until they suit the
concept of each jewelry piece. BETH ROSENGARD

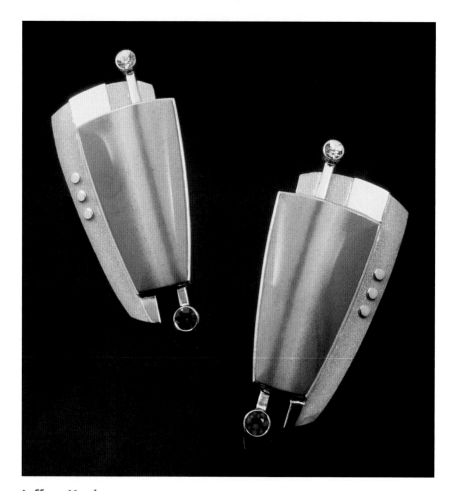

Jeffrey Kaphan

Earrings | 1997

EACH, 5 X 2.5 CM

14-karat yellow gold, 14-karat white
gold, candy jasper, red anthill garnet,
white sapphire; fabricated

PHOTO BY PERRY JOHNSON/IMAGICA

Leila Tai

Blue Iris Earrings | 2005–2006

EACH, 3 X 2.3 X 0.5 CM

18-karat gold, aquamarine, enamel;
hand fabricated, pierced, plique-à-jour

PHOTO BY RALPH GABRINER

Sean and Scott Weaver
Large Boat Earring | 2005
EACH, 4 X 1 X 1.8 CM
18-karat gold, diamonds;
hand fabricated
PHOTO BY HAP SAKWA

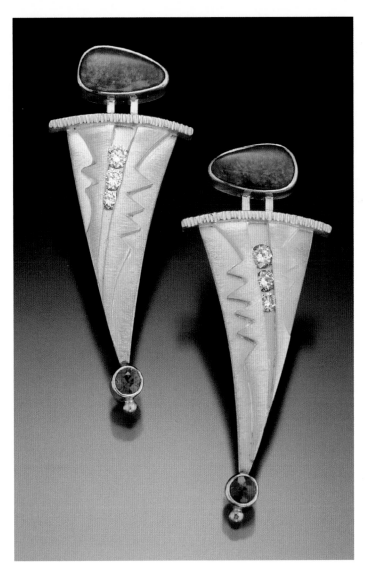

Tami Dean

Untitled | 2000

EACH, 4 X 2 X 0.3 CM

18-karat gold, 14-karat palladium white gold,
opals, diamonds, sapphires; hand fabricated

PHOTO BY HAP SAKWA

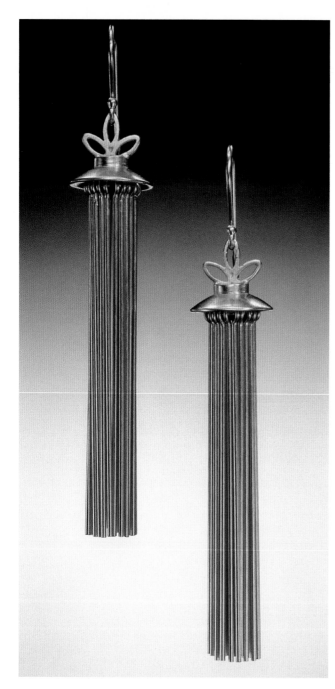

Sayumi Yokouchi
Kanzashi Earring 3 | 2003
EACH, 5.7 X 1 CM
18-karat yellow gold
PHOTO BY RALPH GABRINER

This series was inspired by traditional Japanese hair ornaments, called Kanzash— an extraordinary adornment most commonly used by women during the Edo Period. SAYUMI YOKOUCHI

Polly Wales
Gypsy Wedding | 2005
EACH, 7 X 9 X 0.1 CM
Gold plate, sterling silver, 9-karat
gold, aquamarines; hand pierced
PHOTO BY ARTIST

Barbara Heinrich
Untitled | 2002
EACH, 3.3 X 1 X 1.5 CM
18-karat yellow gold,
diamonds, pearls; pierced
PHOTO BY TIM CALLAHAN

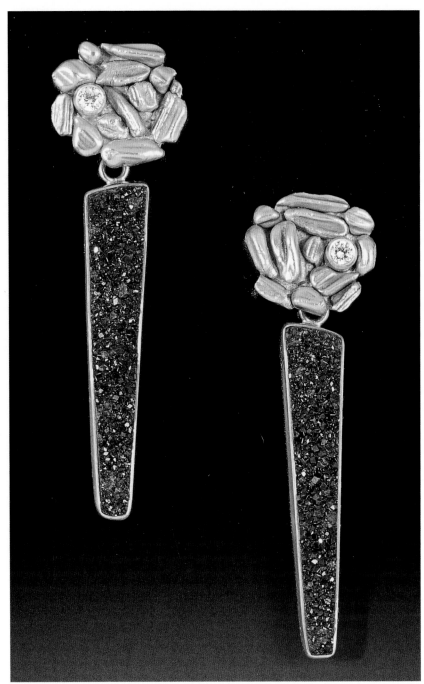

Beth Rosengard
Pebbles | 2004
EACH, 4.1 X 1.6 X 0.5 CM
14-karat gold, 18-karat gold, 22-karat
gold, diamonds, black garnet drusy;
hand fabricated, broom cast
PHOTO BY ARTIST

Michael Good
Untitled | 1981
EACH, 4.4 CM IN DIAMETER
22-karat gold; hand formed, anticlastic
raising, matte finish
PHOTO BY JEFF SLACK

Giovanni Corvaja
Untitled | 2002
EACH, 3.2 X 3.2 X 0.3 CM
18-karat gold, granulation
PHOTO BY ARTIST

Sasha Samuels
Wing Earrings | 2001
EACH, 0.4 X 0.1 X 0.9 CM
Platinum, 18-karat
lemon gold, diamonds
PHOTO BY DANIEL VAN ROSSEN

Abrasha

Untitled | 1994

EACH, 3.8 X 1 CM

18-karat gold, stainless steel, platinum, diamonds; hand fabricated

PHOTO BY ARTIST

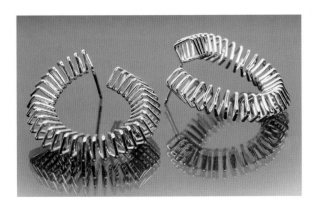

Technique was the starting point—wrapping wire around a square rod to make a square coil. ALAN REVERE

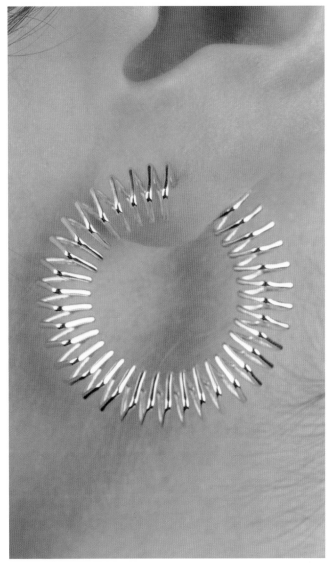

Alan Revere
Untitled | 1984
EACH, 3 X 0.7 CM
14-karat gold; fabricated
PHOTOS BY BARRY BLAU (DETAIL)
AND CHRISTINE DHEIN

Jonathan Hernandez
From the series *Interstellar Bldg. Suite* | 2005
EACH, 13 X 10 CM
Brass
PHOTO BY ROBLY GLOVER

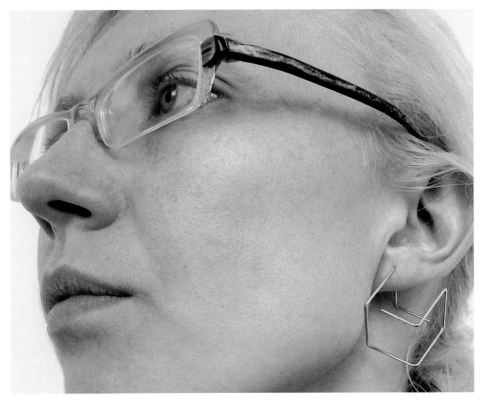

Jiro Kamata
Cube | 2005
EACH, 2 X 2 X 2 CM
18-karat gold
PHOTOS BY ARTIST

Mia Hebib
Dagny Taggart | 2006
EACH, 6.7 X 2.8 X 0.1 CM
Sterling silver; fabricated
PHOTO BY ARTIST AND KEVIN GREVEMBERG

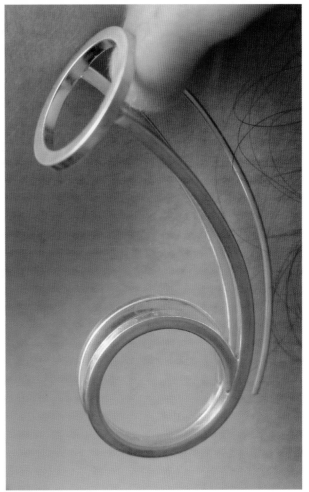

Cheryleve Acosta
Conical Swirl 2 | 2006
EACH, 2 X 3.5 X 1.7 CM
Sterling silver; hand fabricated
PHOTOS BY MICHAEL O'NEILL

Jan Peters

Dimensional Tapered Radius with Pearl Earrings | 2001

EACH, 1.9 X 1.6 X 1.6 CM

Sterling silver, cultured Baroque pearls; hand fabricated, brushed satin finish, burnished

PHOTO BY RALPH GABRINER

Babette Von Dohnanyi

Wing Earrings | 2003

EACH, 3 X 1.2 X 0.4 CM

Sterling silver, rose crystal, patina; cast

PHOTO BY FEDERICO CAVICCHIOLI

Eun Mi Kim
Sorting | 2003
EACH, 4.8 X 3.5 X 3.5 CM
Sterling silver, nylon;
hand fabricated, raised
PHOTO BY PETER NASSOIT

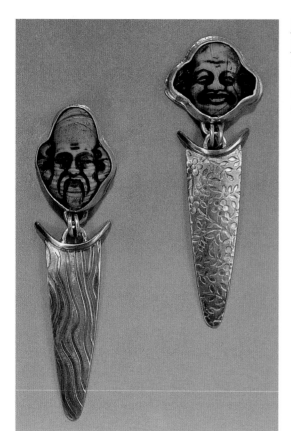

Jan Arthur Harrell
Joy Luck Club | 1998
EACH, 6.4 X 2.5 X 1.3 CM
Polymer clay, sterling
silver, 18-karat gold
PHOTO BY JACK ZILKER

Cappy Counard
Billow Earrings | 2004
EACH, 3.2 X 2.5 X 0.6 CM
18-karat gold, sterling silver, Tibetan
turquoise, patina; hand fabricated,
scored, folded, etched
PHOTO BY ARTIST

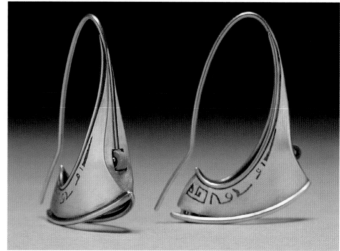

When is wearing a piece of metal next to the skin considered defensive, as in personal armor, or assertive of one's identity, as in a piece of jewelry? This pair of earrings explores the duality of shibuishi, a Japanese alloy traditionally used in swords and furniture, and its current role in contemporary jewelry. LEE RAMSEY HAGA

Lee Ramsey Haga
Japanese Shields | 2001
EACH, 2.7 X 2.2 X 0.3 CM
Shibuishi, 18-karat gold, patina;
reticulated, hand fabricated

PHOTO BY HAP SAKWA
COURTESY OF CONTEMPORARY CRAFTS MUSEUM
AND GALLERY, PORTLAND, OREGON

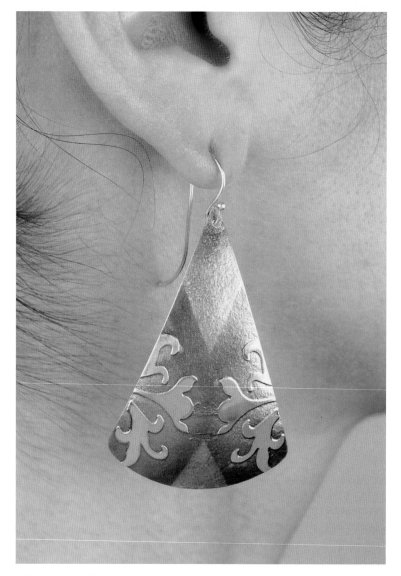

Christine Dhein

Untitled | 2006

EACH, 7.5 X 4 X 1 CM

24-karat gold, sterling silver;
kum boo, roller printed, dapped

PHOTO BY ARTIST

Jill Newbrook

Untitled | 2005

EACH, 5 X 1.3 X 1 CM

18-karat gold, palladium,
silver, pearl

PHOTO BY JÖEL DEGEN

Nanz Aalund

Proto-Type Earrings | 1985

EACH, 5 X 3.5 X 3.5 CM

18-karat gold, sterling silver,
sapphires; hand fabricated

PHOTO BY BOB DRUMM

Influenced by Bauhaus, I made these earrings to balance on the ear so that from the front, one could only see the gold bar with the sapphire arrowhead. Only in profile can one view the full triangular panel. NANZ AALUND

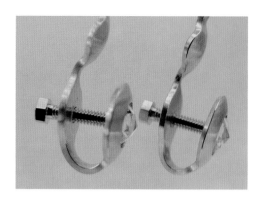

The innovative screw-setting technique allows the wearer to interchange the diamonds with colored stones of a similar cut. LARS SKRODER

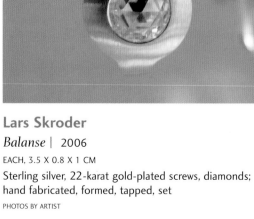

Lars Skroder

Balanse | 2006

EACH, 3.5 X 0.8 X 1 CM

Sterling silver, 22-karat gold-plated screws, diamonds; hand fabricated, formed, tapped, set

PHOTOS BY ARTIST

Françoise and Claude Chavent

Cubes | 1998

EACH, 3.5 X 2.5 X 0.1 CM
Platinum, 18-karat gold; hand fabricated
PHOTO BY ARTISTS

These earrings are entirely flat. The reflection of light over different textures gives the illusion of depth.

CLAUDE AND FRANÇOISE CHAVENT

Venezia Fontana

Once Upon a Time | 2006

LEFT, 1.4 X 1 X 0.6 CM; RIGHT, 2.8 X 1 X 0.3 CM
Silver, 18-karat gold; hand fabricated
PHOTO BY ARTIST

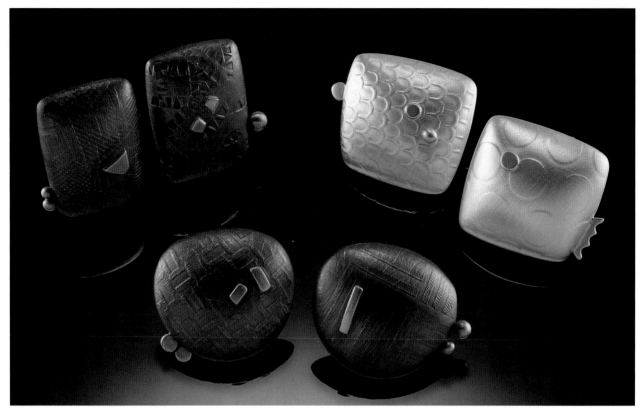

Barbara Bayne
Three Pair of Collage Earrings | 2002
LARGEST, 2 X 2 X 0.5 CM
18-karat gold, sterling silver; die
formed, hand fabricated, oxidized
PHOTO BY PAM PERUGI MARRACCINI

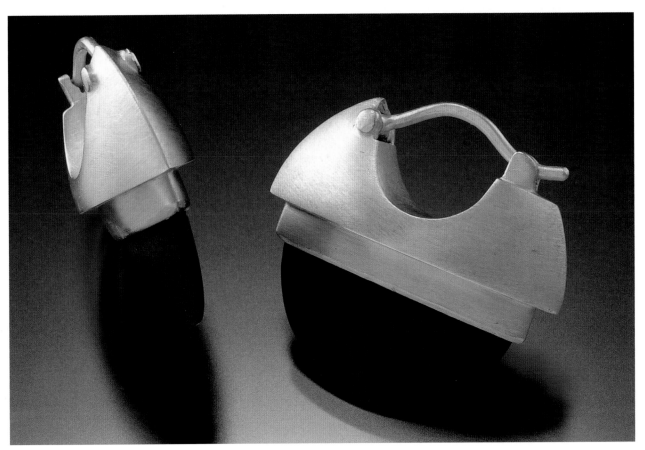

Klaus Spies
Ebony Discus Earrings | 2005
EACH, 3.2 X 3.2 X 0.7 CM
Sterling silver, 18-karat gold,
ebony; hand fabricated
PHOTO BY LARRY SANDERS

Jacqueline Ryan
Untitled | 2000
EACH, 2.8 X 2.2 X 1.4 CM
18-karat palladium white
gold; hand fabricated

PHOTO BY GIOVANNI CORVAJA
COURTESY OF CHARON KRANSEN ARTS,
NEW YORK, NEW YORK

Catherine Hylands
Sail Earrings | 2004
EACH, 2.5 X 1.6 CM
Sterling silver, 18-karat
yellow gold, diamonds
PHOTO BY HAP SAKWA

Reiko Ishiyama
Earrings III | 2003
EACH, 1.6 X 3.5 X 6.7 CM
Sterling silver and 18-karat
gold bimetal; hammer textured,
formed, riveted, oxidized
PHOTO BY CHERRY KIM

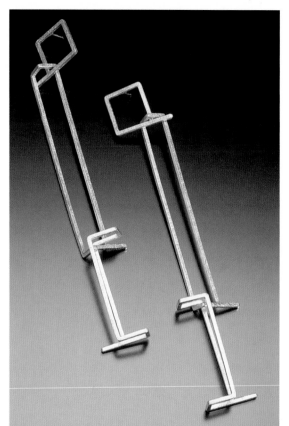

Seth Papac

Corners | 2005

EACH, 11.5 X 2 X 2 CM

18-karat gold, sterling silver,
14-karat gold; fabricated

PHOTO BY DOUG YAPLE

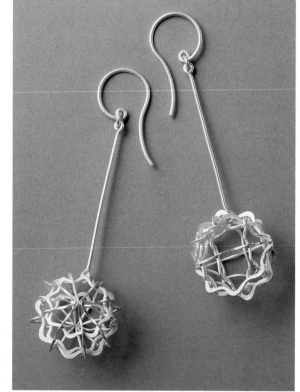

Kirsten Clausager

Flora Con Amore #2 | 2006

EACH, 8 X 2.5 X 2.5 CM

Sterling silver; hand fabricated,
bent, soldered, rolled

PHOTO BY OLE AKHOJ

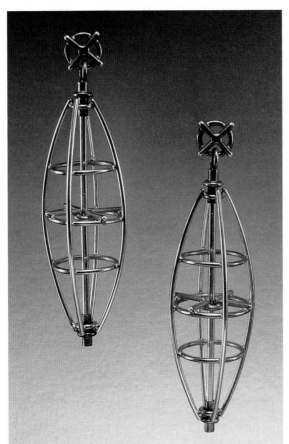

Ben Neubauer
Torpedo Earrings | 2004
EACH, 5.5 X 2 X 2 CM
18-karat gold, sterling silver;
hand fabricated, oxidized
PHOTO BY COURTNEY FRISSE

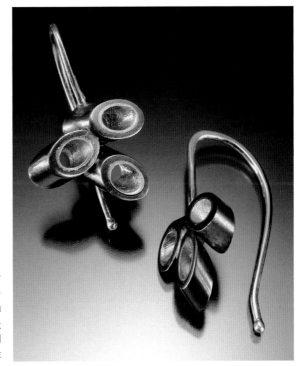

j.e. paterak
Tri Tube Drops | 2004
EACH, 1 X 1 CM
Sterling silver, 18-karat
gold; oxidized
PHOTO BY ROBERT DIAMANTE

Leslie Perrino
On/Off | 2001
EACH, 5 X 3.5 X 1.5 CM
Gold fill, electrical components,
freshwater pearls
PHOTO BY LARRY SANDERS

Lynn Christiansen
Gearrings #1 | 2006
EACH, 6 X 1.5 X 1.5 CM
14-karat gold, sterling silver,
vintage watch parts
PHOTO BY ADRIAN ORDEÑANA

Heidi BigKnife
Untitled | 2004
EACH, 7 X 1.3 X 1.3 CM
Sterling silver, thermoplastic, mailing labels, digital images on paper; hand fabricated, bezel set, inkjet printed
PHOTO BY SCOTT MILLER

Ken Thibado
Light Weight Earrings | 2006
EACH, 5.7 X 1.5 X 1.4 CM
14-karat gold, sapphires, antique pin backs, light bulbs; hand fabricated, bezel set, tube set
PHOTO BY ROBERT DIAMANTE

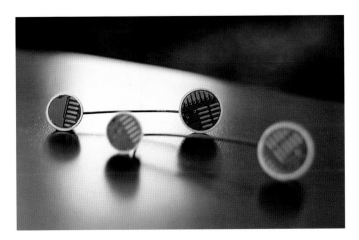

Cindy Kumagai
Untitled | 2006
EACH, 5.7 X 2.5 X 1 CM
Sterling silver, recycled circuit board;
hand fabricated, soldered, oxidized

PHOTOS BY DOUGLAS AMARAL; MODEL, BARBARA WOORTMAN

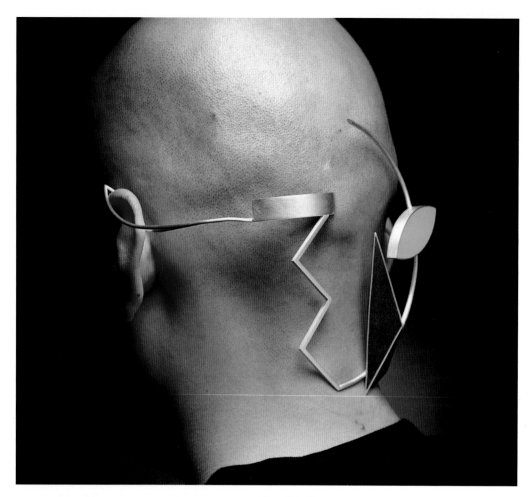

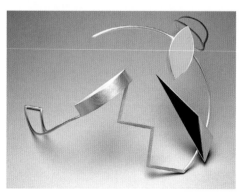

Hea Jin Yang

Stop Backbiting | 2006

14 X 17 X 11 CM

Sterling silver, epoxy
resin; hand fabricated

PHOTOS BY MYUNG-WOOK HUH

N

Marty Jestin
Headspin? | 2004
EACH, 0.4 X 1.3 X 1.2 CM
Automobile dashboard,
acrylic, sterling silver,
18-karat gold; hand fabricated
PHOTO BY ARTIST

Cara Reihberg
Safe? | 2003
8 X 4 X 3 CM
Found materials, car reflector,
television components
PHOTO BY ARTIST

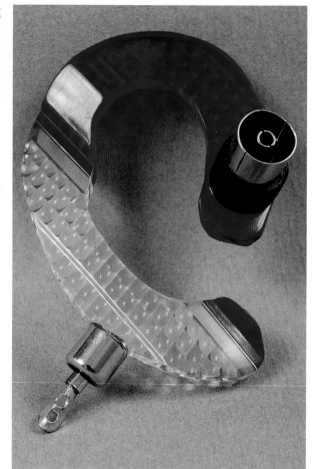

Emiko Oye
Tire Earrings | 2006
EACH, 5.8 X 2.4 X 1.4 CM
Rubber, plastic, cubic zirconia, 14-karat
gold, sterling silver; hand fabricated
PHOTO BY HAP SAKWA

Nostalgic memories or objects from one's childhood often are deemed more precious, invaluable even, than all the gold in one's jewelry box. What if those childhood objects were paired with precious metals and gemstones and made into jewelry? EMIKO OYE

Sungyeoul Lee

Knot So Precious | 2006

13.5 X 5.2 X 3.2 CM

Poly rope, flexible rubber coating;
hand fabricated, dipped

PHOTO BY ARTIST

Lyndsay Rice
Untitled | 2005
LARGEST, 3 X 6 X 0.5 CM
Thermoplastic, silver, ink
PHOTO BY ELLA LA VIGRA

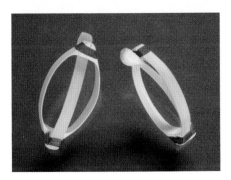

Walter Chen
Untitled | 2005
EACH, 4.5 X 3 X 1.5 CM
Bamboo, nylon thread; sharpened, tied
PHOTOS BY ARTIST

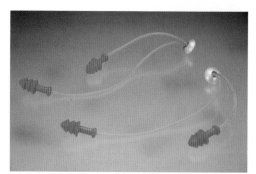

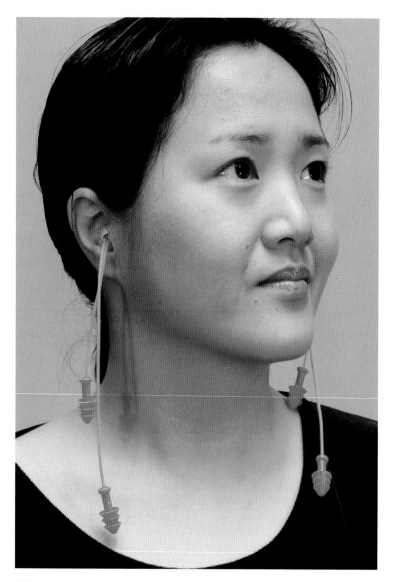

Chieko Arai

I Don't Want To Hearrings | 2006

EACH, 19.7 X 2.5 X 1.7 CM

Silver, plastic, ear plugs;
hand fabricated

PHOTOS BY ARTIST AND SATOMI KAWAI

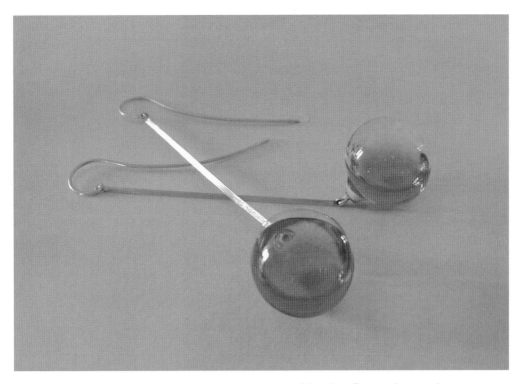

Monica Buongiovanni

Soap Balls | 2006
EACH, 9.5 X 2 X 2 CM
Sterling silver, glass, liquid
soap; hand fabricated
PHOTOS BY ARTIST

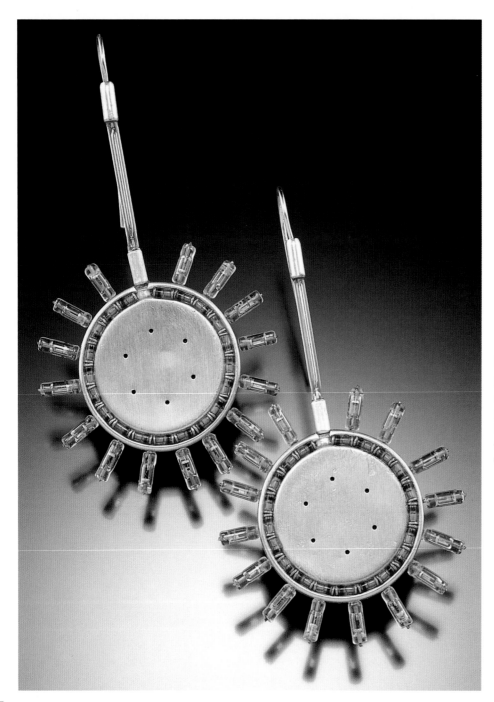

Leslie Perrino
Speakearrings | 2001
EACH, 6.5 X 4 X 0.5 CM
Sterling silver, miniature
headphone speakers,
electrical components
PHOTO BY LARRY SANDERS

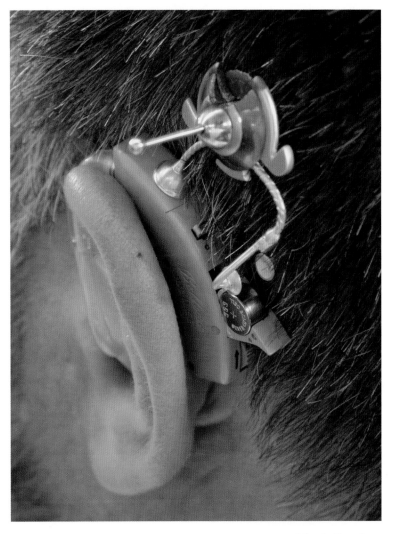

Mark Rooker

Kleptophilus galvanicus | 2006

6 X 6 X 3 CM

Hearing aid, sterling silver, niobium, yellow brass, patina; hand fabricated, anodized, oxidized

PHOTO BY ARTIST

Diana Dudek

Untitled | 2004

EACH, 10 X 2.5 X 0.4 CM

Pearls, pretzels, silver

PHOTO BY SABTISTE COULON

Karen J. Lauseng
Warrior | 2006
EACH, 11 X 2 X 0.5 CM
Toothpicks, 14-karat gold
PHOTO BY ARTIST

Gayle Friedman
Cocoa Pods | 2006
LEFT, 3 X 2.5 CM; RIGHT, 2.7 X 1.9 CM
Sterling silver, dark chocolate, white
chocolate, patina; pierced, hammered
PHOTO BY MARGARET BOOZER

Earlobes are sensual parts of the body. They invite nuzzling and nibbling.
These pieces, which combine my passions for chocolate and jewelry, are
intended to engage as many of the senses as possible. GAYLE FRIEDMAN

191

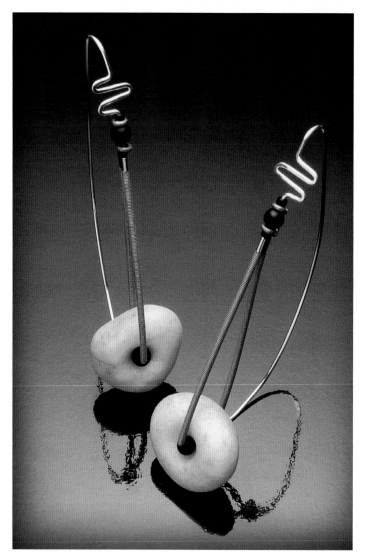

Chris Carlson

From the *Mali Stone* Series | 2006

EACH, 7.5 X 2.5 X 1.3 CM

Neolithic African beads, magnet wire,
onyx, antique African spacers, 14-karat
gold; shaped, hammered

PHOTO BY RYDER GLEDHILL

Julia Converse Sober

Cellular Specimens | 2003

EACH, 6.4 X 1.9 X 1.9 CM

Polymer clay, microscope slides, metal tubing, rubber
O rings, gold-filled wire and beads, metal clay; cane worked

PHOTO BY LARRY SANDERS

These "specimens" combine my two loves—science and art. Thin layers of polymer clay cane slices are sealed under cut glass microscope slides to resemble growing colonies of cells. JULIA CONVERSE SOBER

Louise Fischer Cozzi

Triple Chain Earrings | 2005

EACH, 8.7 X 2.7 X 0.2 CM

Polymer clay, gold, silver leaf, ink, 18-karat
gold, silver, niobium; oxidized

PHOTO BY GEORGE POST

Ruslana Zitserman
Meteorologica: Lightning | 2004
EACH, 7 X 1 X 0.8 CM
Sterling silver, copper, freshwater pearls;
hand fabricated, chain mail, oxidized
PHOTO BY ARTIST

Munya Avigail Upin
Untitled | 1996
EACH, 3.2 X 2.5 X 0.5 CM
Sterling silver, fine silver, copper;
card woven, fabricated
PHOTO BY ARTIST

Joyce Goodman

Fan Earrings | 2006

EACH, 4.5 X 4 X 0.3 CM

22-karat gold, 19-karat gold, sterling silver, copper, patina; hand fabricated, granulation, knitted, sewn

PHOTO BY RALPH GABRINER

Lynn Christiansen
Dinner at 8 | 2006
LONGEST, 18 X 3 X 1.5 CM
14-karat gold, plastic
cutlery, crystals
PHOTO BY ADRIAN ORDEÑANA

Lynn Christiansen
Chandeliearrings | 2005
EACH, 7 X 3 X 3 CM
Silver, cubic zirconia, crystal
briolettes; hand fabricated
PHOTO BY ADRIAN ORDEÑANA

Tom Ferrero

Giraffe Earrings | 2000

EACH, 7 X 2 X 2 CM

Fine silver, 18-karat gold, blue
topaz, patina; fabricated, kum boo

PHOTOS BY DAN NEUBURGER

Kyle H. Leister

Kite Earrings | 2001

EACH, 6.4 X 2.5 X 0.2 CM

Sterling silver, fine silver, copper,
14-karat gold, pearls, patina; fabricated

PHOTO BY ARTIST

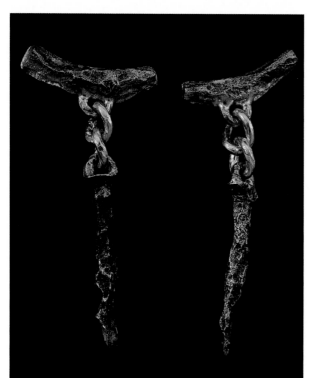

Rob Jackson

Nail Earrings | 2001

EACH, 4 X 2 X 0.5 CM

Iron nail fragments, 18-karat gold,
22-karat gold; hand fabricated

PHOTO BY ARTIST

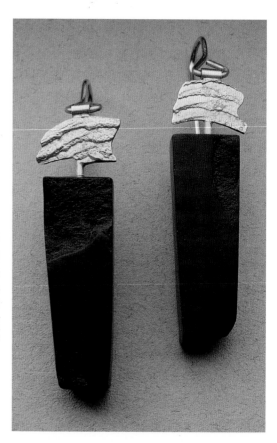

Lee Ramsey Haga

Chance Meeting | 2005

EACH, 5 X 1.2 X 0.7 CM

Shibuishi, 18-karat gold, slate; cuttlebone
cast, hand fabricated, cut, polished

PHOTO BY ARTIST
COURTESY OF CONTEMPORARY CRAFTS
MUSEUM AND GALLERY, PORTLAND, OREGON

*A piece of slate that accidentally split met a cuttlebone
casting, undergoing mitosis in a very zen moment. The
rest is history.* LEE RAMSEY HAGA

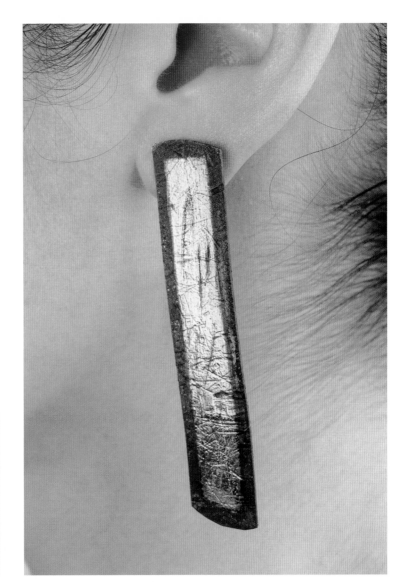

Glenda Ruth

Aki Haiku | 2004

7.5 X 1.5 X 0.1 CM

18-karat gold, silver; fused, carved, roller printed

PHOTOS BY CHRISTINE DHEIN

Adrienne M. Grafton

Chandelier Earrings | 2005

EACH, 9 X 3 X 0.3 CM

Sterling silver, 14-karat gold;
pierced, forged

PHOTO BY TOM MILLS

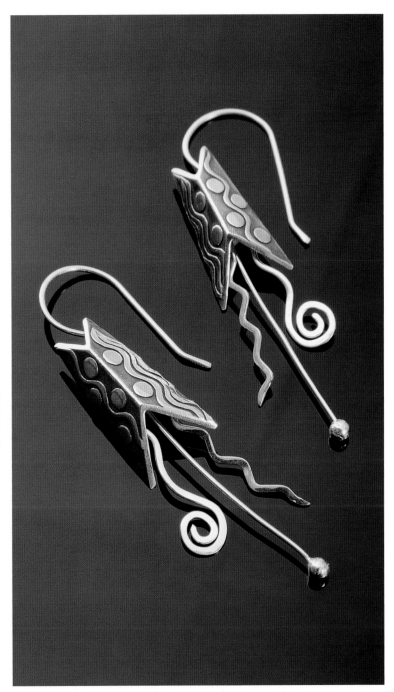

Terry Kovalcik
Dancing Dangles | 2003
EACH, 7 X 1 X 0.7 CM
Metal clay; hand
fabricated, oxidized
PHOTO BY CORRIN KOVALCIK

Kathleen DiResta
Last Leaf, First Snow | 2005
EACH, 7 X 4 X 0.5 CM
Sterling silver, 18-karat gold, shakudo, phantom jasper; formed, fabricated, oxidized
PHOTO BY DEAN POWELL

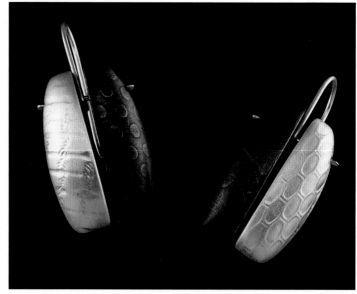

Barbara Bayne
Rectangle Split Earrings | 2001
EACH, 2.3 X 1 X 0.3 CM
Sterling silver; textured, die formed, hand fabricated, oxidized
PHOTO BY PAM PERUGI MARRACCINI

Carol Webb
Half Torii #7 | 1995
EACH, 5.1 X 3.8 X 0.6 CM
Copper clad 22-karat gold
and sterling silver bimetal, pink
tourmaline; etched, oxidized
PHOTO BY RALPH GABRINER

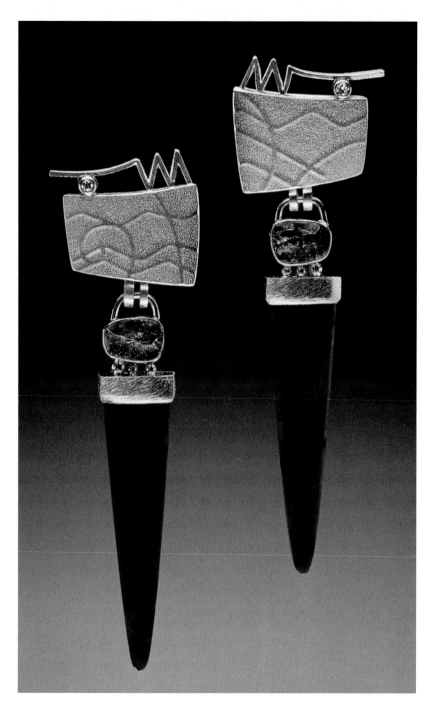

Tami Dean
Untitled | 1994
EACH, 6.4 X 1.9 CM
18-karat gold, 14-karat gold, sugilite, opals, diamonds; roller printed, box construction, soldered
PHOTO BY ARTIST

Janis Kerman

Earrings | 2005

EACH, 3.5 X 2 CM

18-karat yellow gold,
chrysoprase, iolite, pearl,
serpentine; hand fabricated

PHOTO BY DALE GOULD

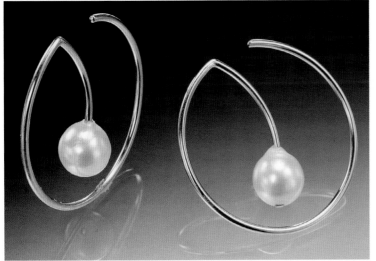

Jan Peters

Cradled Baroque Pearl Hoops | 2000

EACH, 2.5 X 2.5 X 0.4 CM

14-karat gold, cultured Baroque
pearls; hand fabricated, polished

PHOTO BY RALPH GABRINER

*Inserted from the back of the earlobe, the
hoop is rotated and tugged past the narrow
opening between the pearl and wire to rest in the
crook of the earring. The post and security are
integral with its form.* JAN PETERS

Julia Behrends
Overlap Earrings | 2005
EACH, 0.6 X 1.1 X 1.1 CM
Peridot, 18-karat yellow
gold, diamonds; cut, set
PHOTO BY ROBERT DIAMANTE

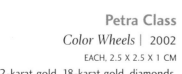

Petra Class
Color Wheels | 2002
EACH, 2.5 X 2.5 X 1 CM
22-karat gold, 18-karat gold, diamonds,
lapis lazuli, tourmaline crystal, garnet,
pearl, citrine; hand fabricated
PHOTO BY HAP SAKWA

Dmitriy Pavlov
Untitled | 2005
EACH, 3.7 X 1.6 X 0.2 CM
18-karat gold, demantoids,
tsavorites, diamonds;
pierced, engraved
PHOTO BY GALINA PAVLOVA

Anna Heindl
Strawberries Long | 2006
EACH, 6.5 X 2.2 X 2.4 CM
18-karat gold, coral
PHOTO BY MAUFRED WAKOLBIUGER

Kirsten Clausager

Flora Con Amore #1 | 2006

EACH, 7 X 2 X 2 CM

18-karat gold, felt, silk string; hand
fabricated, bent, soldered, rolled

PHOTO BY OLE AKHOJ

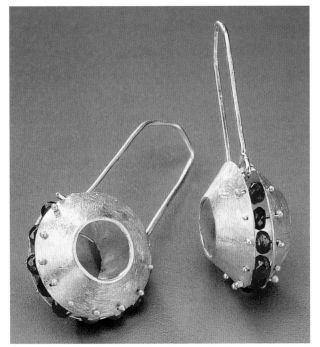

Tamar Kern

Ruby Drop Hoops | 2005

EACH, 4.1 X 1.8 X 1 CM

18-karat gold, rubies

PHOTO BY M. DOYLE
COURTESY OF ALLOY GALLERY,
NEWPORT, RHODE ISLAND

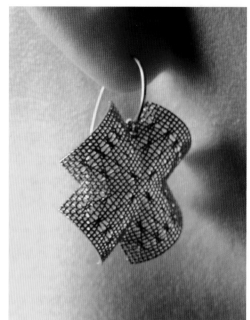

Dennis Nahabetian

Connection Earrings | 2004

Bronze, copper, 14-karat gold, 24-karat
gold plate; electroformed, fabricated

PHOTOS BY ARTIST; MODEL, DIANA RUPP

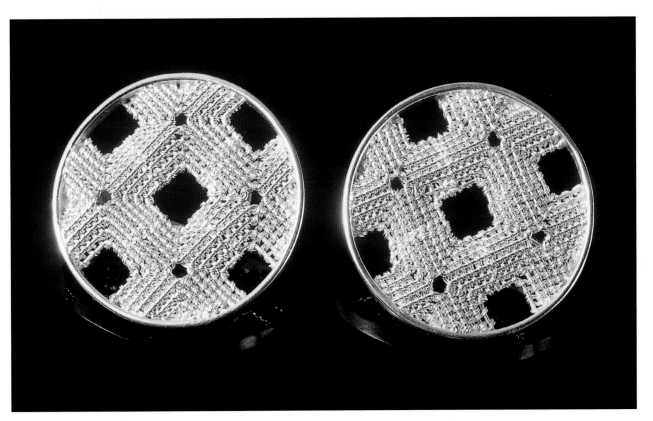

Mary Lee Hu
Earrings #165 | 1997
EACH, 2.8 X 2.8 X 1.5 CM
18-karat gold, 22-karat gold;
twined, fabricated
PHOTO BY ARTIST

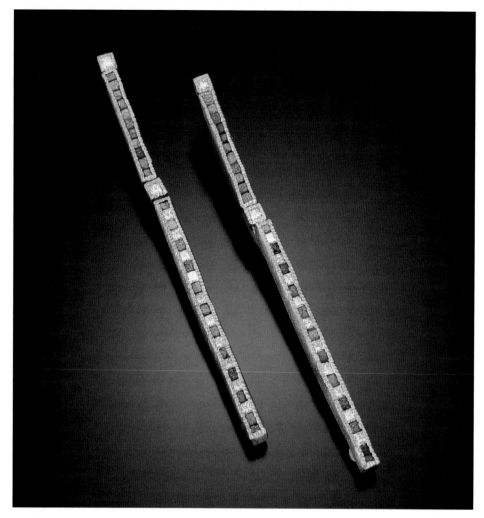

Todd Reed

Untitled | 2004

EACH, 3.8 X 0.3 X 0.3 CM

22-karat yellow gold, 18-karat
yellow gold, sterling silver, raw
diamonds, cut diamonds, patina;
hand forged, fabricated

PHOTO BY AZAD

Sean and Scott Weaver

X Pod Square Earring | 2005

EACH, 6 X 1.5 X 1.5 CM

18-karat gold,
diamonds; fabricated

PHOTO BY HAP SAKWA

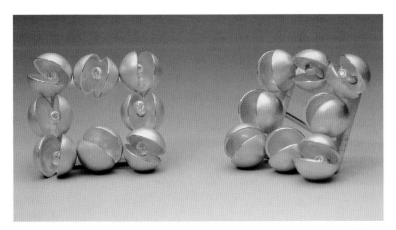

Liaung-Chung Yen

Untitled | 2006

EACH, 1.8 X 1.8 X 0.8 CM

18-karat gold, diamonds

PHOTO BY ARTIST

The balls are loosely attached, creating movement and sound. LIAUNG-CHUNG YEN

Barbara Heinrich

Untitled | 1990

EACH, 6.2 X 2.5 X 1 CM

18-karat yellow gold, diamonds, pearls;
chased, hand fabricated, bezel set

PHOTO BY TIM CALLAHAN

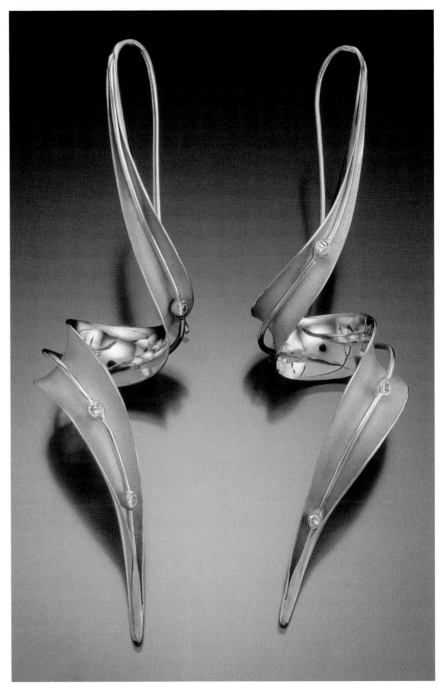

Jerry Scavezze
Orbits | 1998
EACH, 4 X 2 X 2 CM
18-karat gold, platinum,
diamonds; anticlastic
raising, fabricated
PHOTO BY RALPH GABRINER

I like the play of light on the different surfaces as well as the orbiting platinum wire. JERRY SCAVEZZE

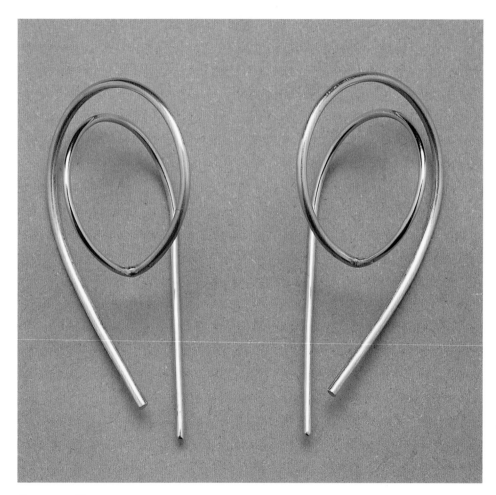

Suzanne Esser
Untitled | 2004
EACH, 3.3 X 1 CM
14-karat gold
PHOTO BY RON ZÜLSHA

Dana Melnick
Live Wire Peace Earrings | 2006
EACH, 5 X 4.5 X 0.1 CM
14-karat gold wire; heated, hand bent
PHOTO BY SANDRA RODGERS

219

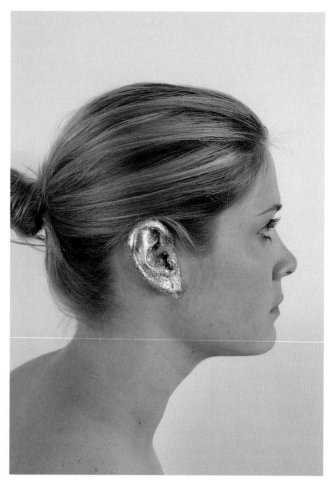

Gabriel Craig
Untitled | 2006
4.5 X 3 X 1 CM
23-karat gold leaf; temporary
site-specific adornment
PHOTO BY AMY E. WEIKS

Mary Preston
Bobbin Lace Earrings | 2004
EACH, 4.7 X 3.1 X 0.5 CM
18-karat gold, pana shell;
hand fabricated

PHOTO BY ARTIST
COURTESY OF ORNAMENTUM GALLERY,
HUDSON, NEW YORK

Hu Jun
Untitled | 2006
EACH, 20 X 10 X 2 CM
Paper pulp, brass;
hand fabricated

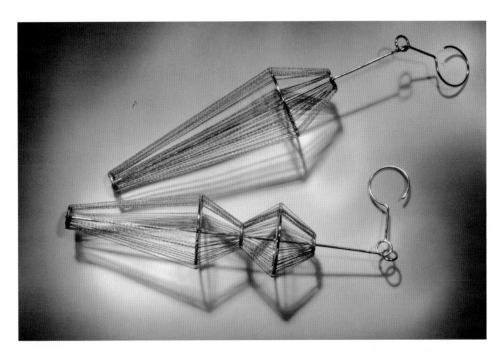

Rudee Tancharoen
Untitled | 2005
EACH, 8 X 2 X 2 CM
White gold, silk thread
PHOTO BY ARTIST

Jennifer W. Chachenian

Hair | 2005

EACH, 8 X 2 X 0.3 CM

Copper, sterling silver,
enamel; hand fabricated

PHOTO BY MARK JOHNSTON

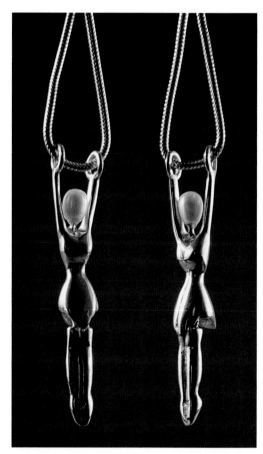

Kristin Noakes

Flying Trapeze | 2005

EACH, 10 X 1 CM

Sterling silver, pearls

PHOTO BY ARTIST

Emily McLoughlin
Imprisoned Glimmer | 2006
10 X 7.5 X 0.2 CM
Copper, sterling silver, epoxy
resin, glitter; formed, soldered
PHOTO BY ARTIST

Elizabeth Glass Geltman
Pink Paper Fantasy 1 | 2006
EACH, 6 X 4 CM
Copper, rubber, paper;
formed, hand fabricated
PHOTO BY ARTIST

I like to create beautiful things out of unexpected objects. These earrings combine pink copy paper, discarded rubber, and scrap copper sheet and wire. The fantasy is achieving recycling at its best—creating something beautiful, in this case jewelry, out of trash. ELIZABETH GLASS GELTMAN

Hans-Erwin Leicht
Untitled | 2000
EACH, 4.5 X 2.5 CM
Silver, brass, patina;
hand fabricated
PHOTO BY ARTIST

Tessa E. Rickard

Rhinestone Baby | 2006

7.6 X 3.2 X 2.5 CM

Plastic, sterling silver, cubic
zirconia; hand fabricated

PHOTO BY TIM CARPENTER

Kaz Robertson
Mis-match Magnet Earrings | 2005
LONGEST, 9 CM
Resin, magnets, silver chain
PHOTO BY ARTIST

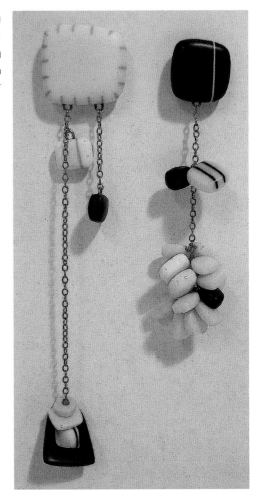

Magnets set within resin allows the wearer to stick the earrings into various positions, making them very versatile and playful. KAZ ROBERTSON

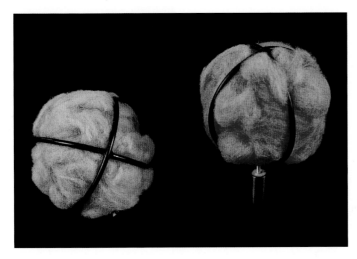

Laura Coddens
Untitled | 2006
EACH, 2 X 2 X 3.5 CM
Steel, sterling silver, cotton, dye, rubber; hand fabricated
PHOTO BY AMY WEIKS

Felieke van der Leest

The Ostricheez | 2003

ON BASE, EACH 8.5 X 5.5 X 5.5 CM; AS WORN, 7 X 3 X 3 CM

Yarn, plastic toy, gold, gravel, cubic zirconia; crocheted

PHOTOS BY EDDO HARTMANN

Barbi Gossen
Untitled | 2006
EACH, 6 X 2.5 X 2.5 CM
Gold, sterling silver, fine silver,
enamel; raised, sifted, cloisonné
PHOTO BY ARTIST

Nikolay Sardamov

Earrings | 2006

FROM 3 X 3 X 2 CM TO 3 X 4 X 4 CM

Alpaca, glass beads, silicon;
etched, assembled

PHOTO BY ANGEL PENCHEV

Yuzuka Oguro

Trapped | 2006

EACH, 3 X 3 X 1 CM

Fine silver, sterling silver, cubic
zirconia; hand fabricated, soldered

PHOTO BY ARTIST

Jessica Davies

Blue Brush Earrings | 2005

EACH, 4.5 X 2.5 CM

Sterling silver, stainless steel,
chenille; fabricated, soldered

PHOTO BY DON FELTON

233

Silina Pantelidou
Untitled | 2006
5.5 X 2 X 0.5 CM
Silver, paper, paint, steel wire
PHOTO BY STAVROS NIFLIS

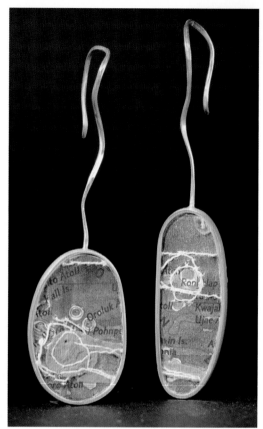

Jessee J. Smith
Organelles | 2006
EACH, 6 X 3.1 X 0.5 CM
Sterling silver, copper, patina;
pierced, textured, soldered
PHOTO BY ARTIST

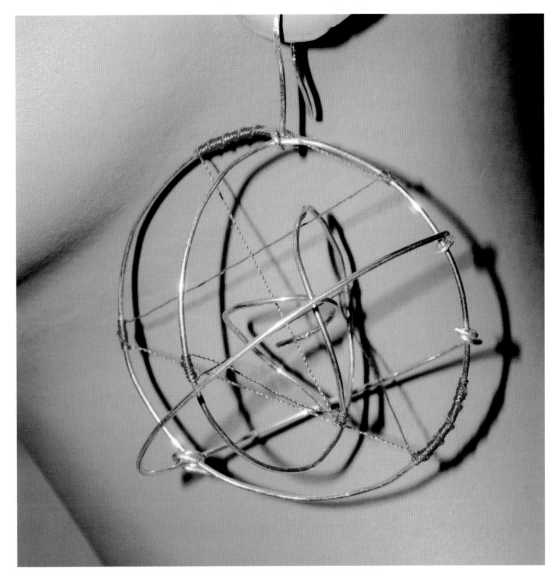

Madeline Reed
Orbital | 2006
7.3 X 5 X 4 CM
Sterling silver, thread
PHOTO BY ARTIST

Helen Ellison-Dorion
Untitled | 2003
EACH, 7 X 2.5 X 2.5 CM
Sterling silver, fine silver, patina,
enamel; hand fabricated
PHOTO BY ARTIST

Sarah Hood
Padme Earrings | 1999
EACH, 3.5 X 1.3 X 1.3 CM
Sterling silver, 18-karat
yellow gold
PHOTO BY DOUG YAPLE

Marjorie Simon
Green Lantern Earrings | 2005
EACH, 7 X 2 X 1 CM
Enamel, fine silver, 22-karat gold
bimetal, sterling silver, freshwater pearl
PHOTO BY RALPH GABRINER

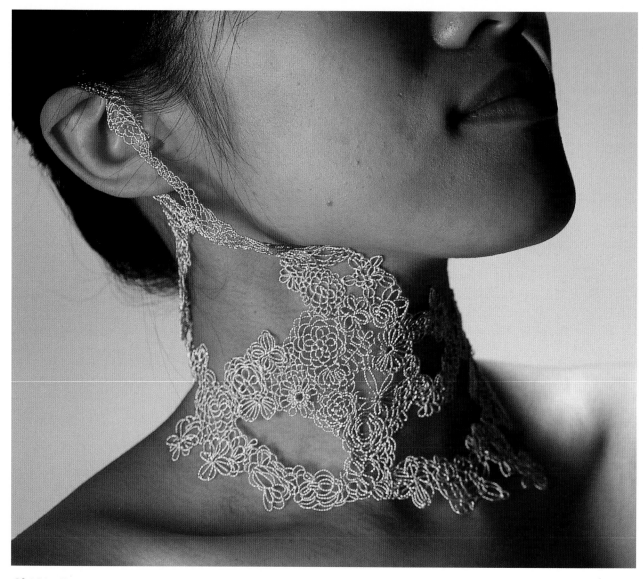

Chi Yu-Fang

Laced with Lace | 2006

20 X 10 X 20 CM

Silver; twisted

PHOTO BY ARTIST

Michelle Chan
Personal Space | 2006
EACH, 21.9 X 4.4 X 6.6 CM
Sterling silver, cubic zirconia,
rubber cord; hand fabricated
PHOTO BY ARTIST

Amy Weiks
Untitled | 2006
2.5 X 2.5 X 1 CM
Sterling silver; hand fabricated
PHOTO BY ARTIST

Verónica Alonso
Spindles | 2006
EACH, 6.5 X 0.7 X 0.7 CM
Sterling silver, fine
silver; hand fabricated
PHOTO BY ARTIST

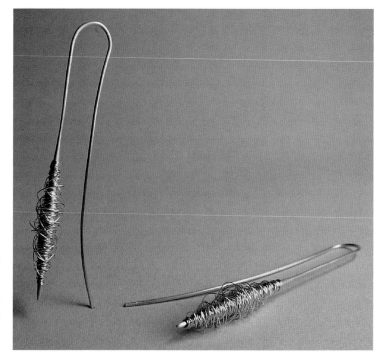

Munya Avigail Upin

Hyperbola Plugs | 2006

EACH, 4 X 4 X 3 CM

Silver, pearl, foam ear plugs;
crocheted, fabricated

PHOTO BY ARTIST

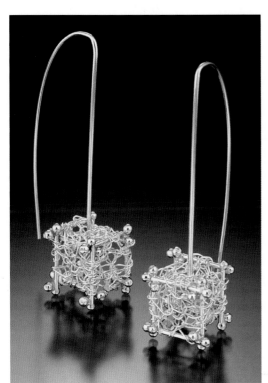

Randi S. Chervitz

Cube Earrings | 2003

EACH, 6 X 1.2 X 2.5 CM

Sterling silver, fine silver
wire; fabricated, crocheted

PHOTO BY HAP SAKWA

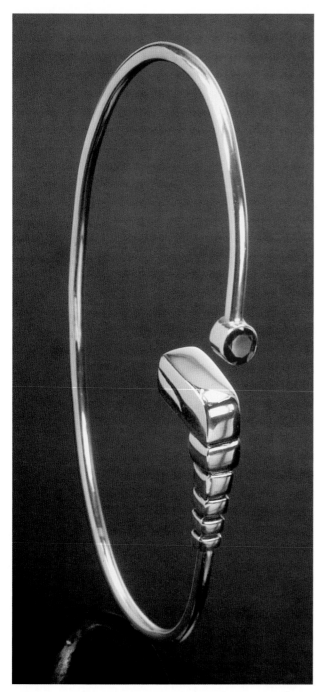

Danielle Crampsie
Headphone Earpiece | 2003
5 X 0.5 X 4 CM
Sterling silver, synthetic ruby; wax
carved, cast, hand fabricated
PHOTO BY PAUL AMBTMAN

*This piece, meant to blend man and machine, comments
on the lack of unity within our culture. Personal listening
devices remove you from your situation, causing you to be no
longer engaged in your surroundings, and therefore, breaking
the bond between you and those sharing your space. The case
component in the piece references the headphone jack in a
portable stereo. The idea being that you are plugged into
yourself.* DANIELLE CRAMPSIE

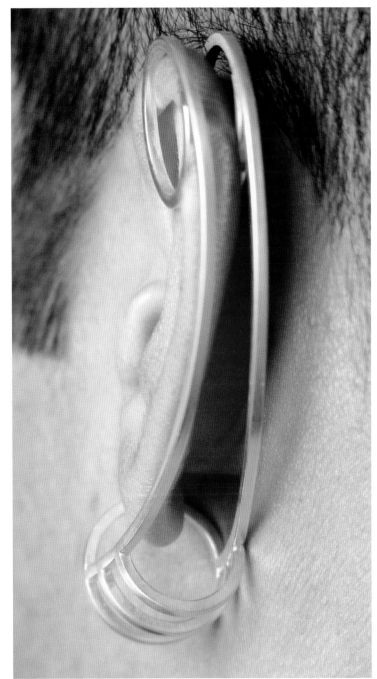

Cheryleve Acosta
Ear Brooch | 2006
2.8 X 7.5 X 1.9 CM
Sterling silver; hand fabricated
PHOTOS BY MICHAEL O'NEILL

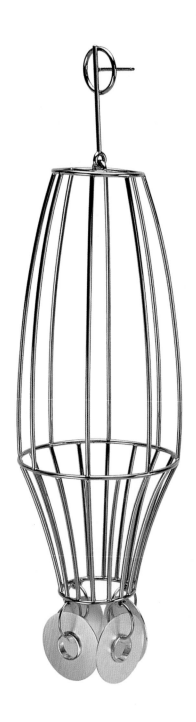
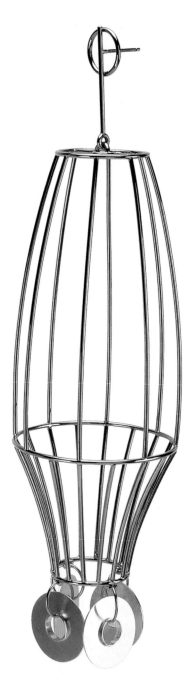

Rachelle Thiewes
Shimmer | 2004
EACH, 13.6 X 3.6 X 3.6 CM
18-karat palladium white gold, silver
PHOTO BY ARTIST

Sim Luttin
Wishes | 2006
EACH, 5 X 2 X 2 CM
Fine silver; forged
PHOTO BY KEVIN MONTAGUE

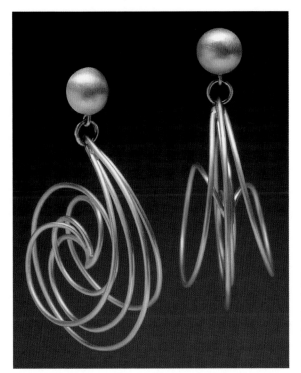

Jennifer Bauser
Untitled | 2006
EACH, 7 X 3 X 4.5 CM
Sterling silver; hand fabricated,
hollow construction, satin finish
PHOTO BY DOUG YAPLE

Karin Kato

The Water Formed into Icicles | 2006

LARGEST, 6.8 X 2 X 2.5 CM

Sand, resin, silver

PHOTO BY ARTIST

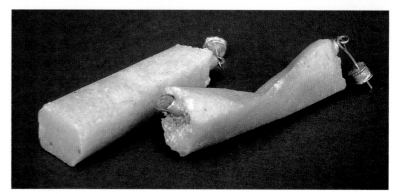

Yuka Saito

Untitled | 2006

12 X 4.5 X 4.5 CM

Recycled polypropylene,
polyurethane, sterling silver

PHOTO BY ARTIST

Johan Van Aswegen
Fleur De Lys Earrings
Enamel, 18-karat gold; inlay, set
PHOTO BY ARTIST

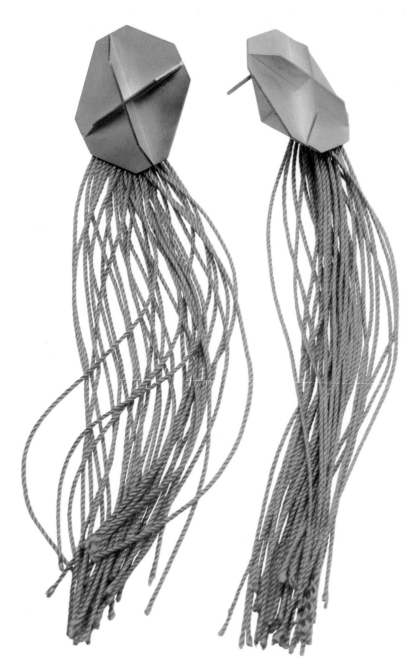

Rebecca Deans
Graduate | 2006
EACH, 11.5 X 2 X 1.5 CM
Sterling silver, silk;
hand fabricated
PHOTO BY BRIAN STEVENS

K.C. Calum
Granite Earrings #2 | 2006
EACH, 8 X 4.5 X 1.5 CM
Wood, rubber, paint
PHOTO BY ARTIST

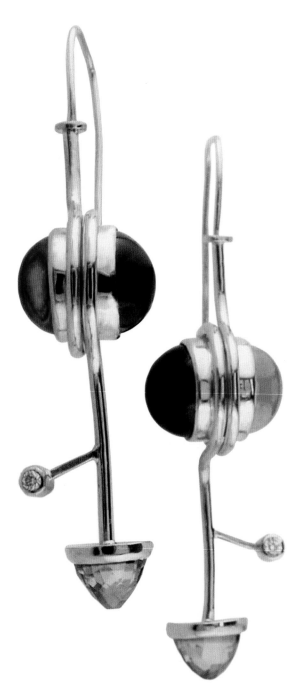

Jessica Baneham

Atomic Earrings | 2006

EACH, 7.5 X 1.5 X 1.5 CM

18-karat yellow gold, 18-karat white gold, amethyst, citrine, topaz, diamond; hand fabricated, soldered construction, bezel set, tube set

PHOTO BY ARTIST

Claude Schmitz
Madeleine | 2006
EACH, 4.4 X 1.8 X 1.3 CM
18-karat gold, turquoise;
hand fabricated
PHOTO BY WIM

Anna Heindl

Motors | 2001

EACH, 2.3 X 2 X 3.6 CM

18-karat gold, fire opals

PHOTO BY MAUFRED WAKOLBIUGER

Heather Guidero

Interlocking Ellipse Earrings | 2006

EACH, 5.5 X 1 X 1 CM

22-karat gold and sterling silver
bimetal; hand fabricated

PHOTO BY KELLI RUGGERE

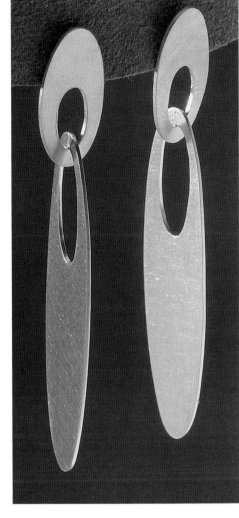

Terry Kovalcik

Untitled | 2005

EACH, 6.2 X 2 CM

Metal clay, sterling silver, black
opal, golden sapphire, moonstone

PHOTO BY CORRIN KOVALCIK

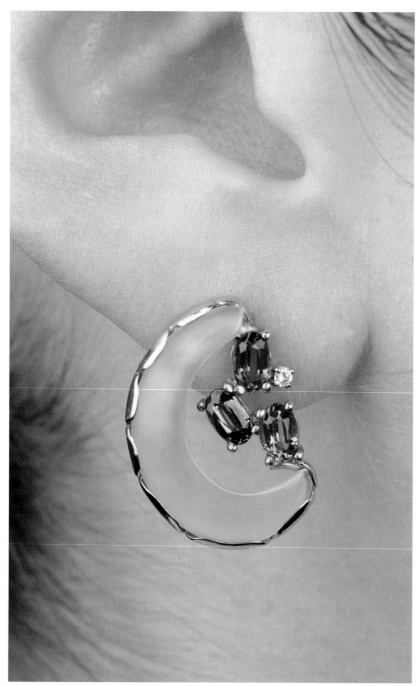

PHOTO BY CHRISTINE DHEIN

John Donivan
Free Fall | 2001
2.2 X 1.7 X 0.3 CM
18-karat yellow gold, quartz,
spinels, diamonds; hand carved,
fabricated, prong set, split bezels
PHOTO BY CHRISTINE DHEIN

Brent R. Keeney
Sapphire Stripes | 2004
EACH, 3 X 1.5 X 0.5 CM
18-karat gold, 14-karat gold, sapphires,
diamonds; hand fabricated
PHOTO BY ARTIST

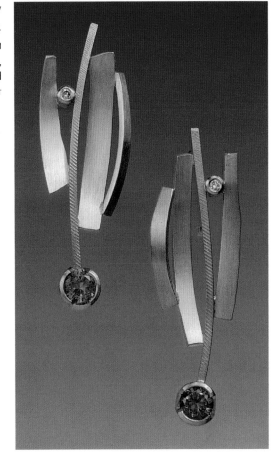

Dana Melnick
Cono Spinner Earrings | 2005
EACH, 5 X 2 CM
18-karat yellow gold, pink tourmalines;
lost wax cast, hand fabricated, bezel set
PHOTO BY HAP SAKWA

*Head movements cause these earrings
to spin when worn.* DANA MELNICK

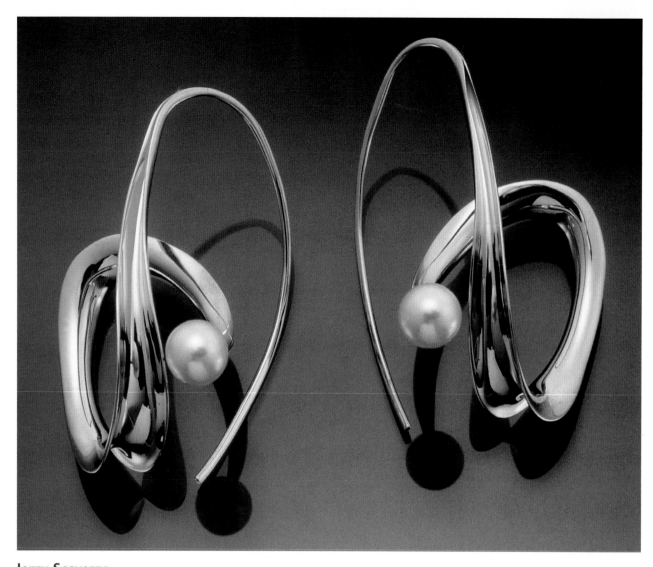

Jerry Scavezze

Tango | 2001

EACH, 4 X 2.5 X 1.5 CM

14-karat gold, pearls;
anticlastic raising

PHOTO BY RALPH GABRINER

Natasha Wozniak

Spiral Foliage Earrings | 2005

EACH, 5 X 1.6 X 1 CM

18-karat gold, 22-karat gold,
tourmalines; repoussé, cut,
soldered, bezel set

PHOTO BY RALPH GABRINER

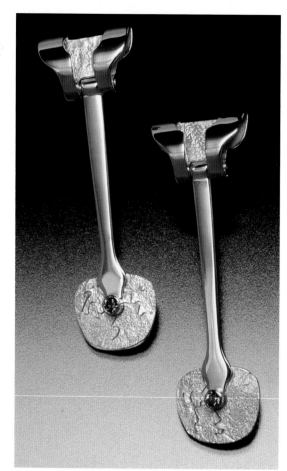

Joan Tenenbaum

Tidepool Earrings | 2004

EACH, 3.8 X 1.3 X 1.3 CM

18-karat green gold, 18-karat yellow gold, 18-karat palladium white gold, diamonds; hand fabricated, granulation, pierced, formed, hinged, riveted

PHOTO BY DOUG YAPLE

Ronda Coryell

Untitled | 2005

EACH, 3 X 2 CM

22-karat gold, platinum, rainbow moonstones; granulation

PHOTO BY CHRISTINE DHEIN

Karen Mitchell, Karen Mitchell Design
Untitled | 2005
EACH, 9 X 1 CM
22-karat gold, freshwater pearl,
aquamarines; granulation
PHOTO BY ARTIST

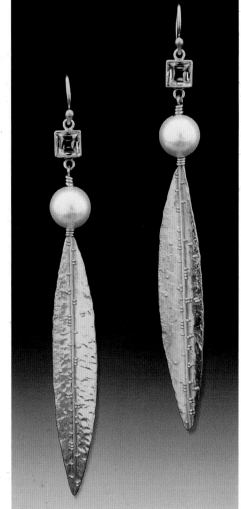

Antje Roitzsch
Persephone Earrings | 1996
EACH, 5 X 2.5 X 1.5 CM
18-karat gold; anticlastic raising,
polished, matte finished
PHOTO BY JEFF SLACK

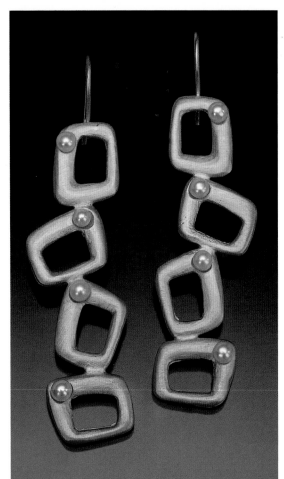

Jennifer Bauser
Untitled | 2006

EACH, 6.5 X 1.5 X 0.2 CM

24-karat vermeil, sterling silver, freshwater pearls; carved, cast, satin finish

PHOTO BY DOUG YAPLE

Roberta Ann Weisenburg
Untitled | 1999

EACH, 5.1 X 1.3 X 1.3 CM

22-karat gold, pearl, citrine, 18-karat gold; hand fabricated, granulation

PHOTO BY GEORGE POST

Nina Basharova
Milky Way Day and Night Earrings | 2006

EACH, 4.5 X 3.8 X 0.8 CM

18-karat gold, diamonds

PHOTO BY DYLAN CROSS

Detachable for day and evening wear. NINA BASHAROVA

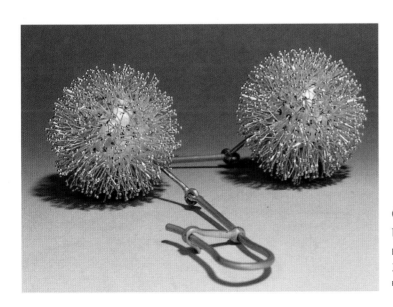

Giovanni Corvaja
Untitled | 1998

EACH, 1.8 X 1.8 X 1.8 CM

22-karat gold

PHOTO BY ARTIST

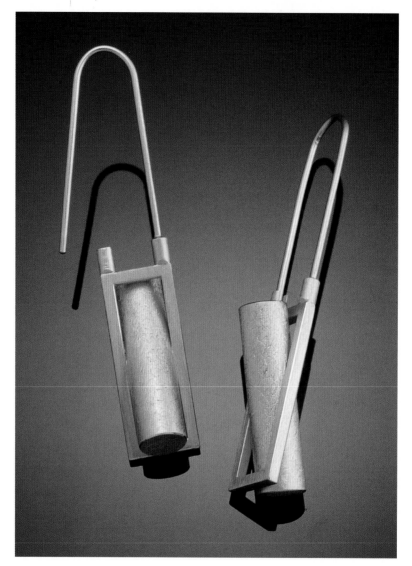

Geoffrey D. Giles

Boxed Angled One Tube | 2006

EACH, 5.1 X 1 X 1.3 CM

18-karat yellow gold, 18-karat white
gold; hollow form fabricated, brushed
finish, surface embellished

PHOTO BY TAYLOR DABNEY

Giovanni Corvaja
Untitled | 2003
EACH, 3.2 X 3.2 X 1.2 CM
18-karat gold; soldered, niello
PHOTO BY ARTIST

George Sawyer

Mokume Puff Earrings | 2006

EACH, 6.5 X 1.8 X 1.8 CM

14-karat mokume gane,
14-karat gold; hand fabricated

PHOTO BY ARTIST

Thomas Herman

Acanthus Squares | 2005

EACH, 2.7 X 1.4 X 1.2 CM

18-karat yellow gold, diamonds; carved, pierced, chased, engraved, inlay, set

PHOTO BY RALPH GABRINER

Belle Brooke Barer

Boat Earrings | 2006

EACH, 2.6 X 2.4 X 0.4 CM

18-karat yellow gold, sterling silver, synthetic diamond; hand fabricated

PHOTO BY ARTIST

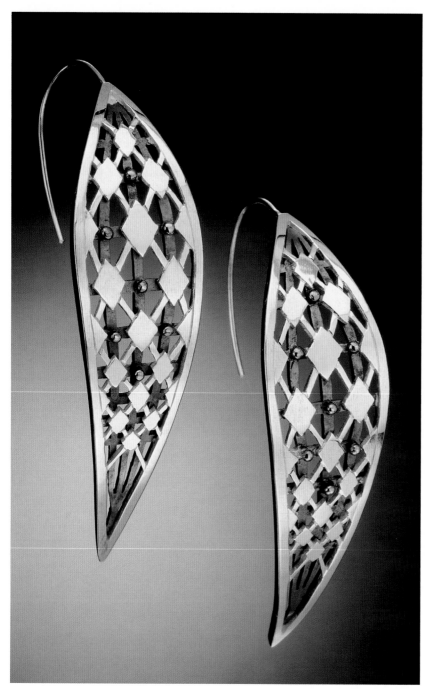

Jessica Scofield

Trellis Earrings | 2006

EACH, 5 X 1.4 X 2.7 CM

18-karat gold, sterling silver; fabricated, pierced, engraved, oxidized

PHOTO BY HAP SAKWA

I am intrigued by the surface of things, how surface pattern reveals the underlying structure. The Trellis Earrings *design originated in studies of steel bridge supports that expand and contract with the span of the bridge. The gentle curve of the earrings appears to stretch and distort the trellis pattern in a similar way.* JESSICA SCOFIELD

Jayne Redman
Columbine Earrings | 2003
EACH, 4.2 X 2 X 2 CM
18-karat yellow gold, 18-karat
white gold, sterling silver; hand
fabricated, oxidized
PHOTO BY ROBERT DIAMANTE

Yoshiko Yamamoto

Ear-Rings Kinetic | 2005

EACH, 4 X 4.5 X 0.6 CM

Sterling silver, 18-karat gold;
hand fabricated

PHOTO BY DEAN POWELL

Reiko Ishiyama

Earrings I | 2001

EACH, 7 X 3.2 X 1.9 CM

Sterling silver and 18-karat gold
bimetal; hammer textured,
pierced, riveted, formed, oxidized

PHOTO BY RALPH GABRINER

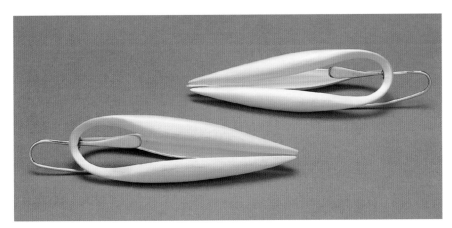

Suzanne Esser

Swan | 2003

EACH, 6.5 X 1.7 CM

Silver, 14-karat gold; chased

PHOTO BY RON ZÜLSHA

Abrasha
Untitled | 1995
EACH, 2 X 0.7 CM
18-karat gold, 24-karat gold, stainless steel, diamonds; hand fabricated
PHOTO BY ARTIST

Françoise and Claude Chavent
Copeaux | 2005
EACH, 3.5 X 2.5 X 0.1 CM
Platinum, 22-karat gold;
hand fabricated
PHOTO BY ARTISTS

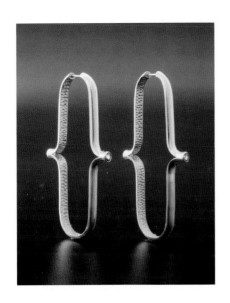

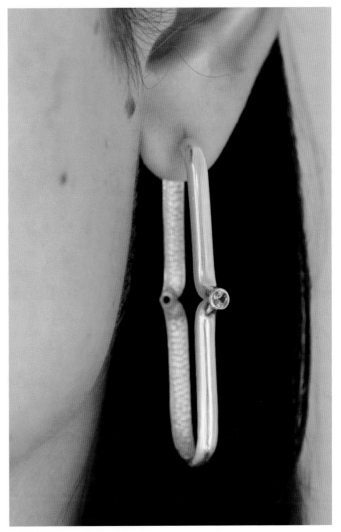

Derek McKay Duncan
Untitled | 2006
EACH, 8 X 4 X 1 CM
Sterling silver, 24-karat gold plating,
tsavorite garnets; hand fabricated
PHOTOS BY ARTIST

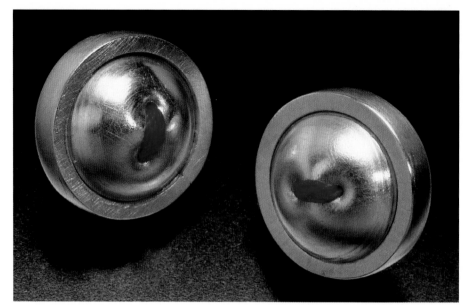

Rosemary Pham
Button Earrings | 2005
EACH, 1.3 X 1.3 X 0.7 CM
Sterling silver, embroidery
floss; hand fabricated

PHOTO BY DOUG YAPLE
COURTESY OF FACÈRÉ JEWELRY ART GALLERY,
SEATTLE, WASHINGTON

Elizabeth Bone
Untitled | 2005
EACH, 4.5 X 3.5 CM
Silver; hand fabricated
PHOTO BY JOËL DEGEN

Mizuko Yamada
Earrings with Fluttering in Flakes | 2000
5.5 X 3.6 X 3.6 CM
18-karat gold, silver;
raised, soldered
PHOTO BY TOSHIHIDE KAJIHARA

John Wik
Intergalactic Star Chambers | 2006
EACH, 5 X 2.5 X 1 CM
Anodized aluminum valve caps,
bolt, argentium sterling silver
PHOTO BY CHRIS WIK

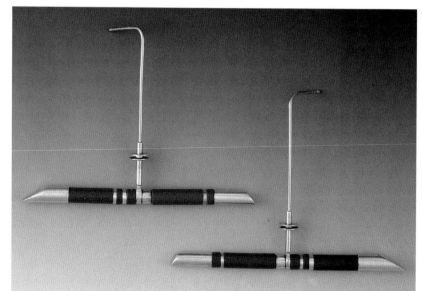

Dorothea Hosom
Untitled | 2005
EACH, 4.1 X 5.6 X 4 CM
Sterling silver, white gold, copper
wire insulation; fabricated
PHOTO BY ARTIST

Hyeseung Shin
One Day in My Childhood | 2003
EACH, 5 X 3 X 1 CM
Sterling silver
PHOTO BY MUNCH

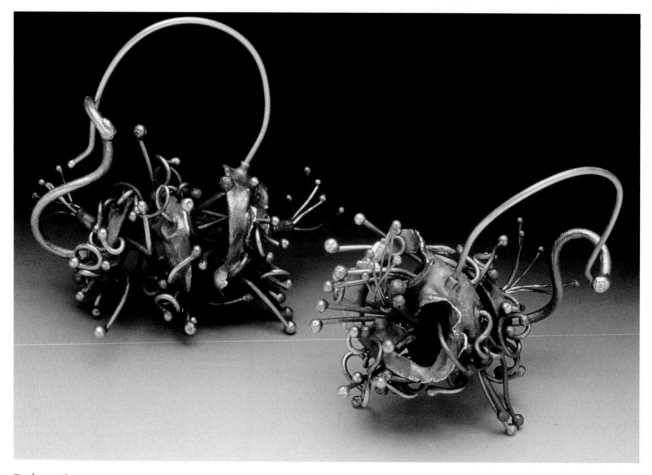

Robert Longyear
Destructo Swarmbots | 2003
EACH, 4 X 3 X 4 CM
Sterling silver, copper; chased,
repoussé, fabricated
PHOTO BY DON CASPER

Lauren Debus

Phantasmagoria | 2004

6 X 5 X 2.5 CM

Copper, silver; hand
fabricated, forged, riveted

PHOTO BY ARTIST

Jessica Jacobi
Untitled | 2006
9 X 4 X 3 CM
Silver, patina; forged, soldered
PHOTO BY BOB MOSIER

Philip Sajet

Spike Earrings | 1986

EACH, 7 X 2 X 2 CM

Silver; oxidized

PHOTO BY ARTIST

Katrina LaPenne

Claw Earrings | 2004

EACH, 7 X 6 X 2.5 CM

Sterling silver; hand fabricated
and formed, oxidized

PHOTO BY MARTY DOYLE

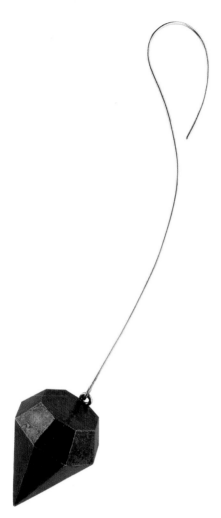

Yoko Shimizu
Untitled | 2005
8 X 2 X 2 CM
Silver, 18-karat gold;
hand fabricated, niello
PHOTO BY FEDERICO CAVICCHIOLI

Donna E. Shimazu
Articulated Flower Cascade Series | 2005
EACH, 5.4 X 1.3 CM
Shibuishi, 14-karat green gold,
14-karat yellow gold, patina; cast,
fabricated, riveted, engraved, torch painted
PHOTO BY JENNIFER CASTILLO

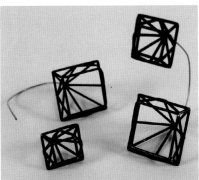

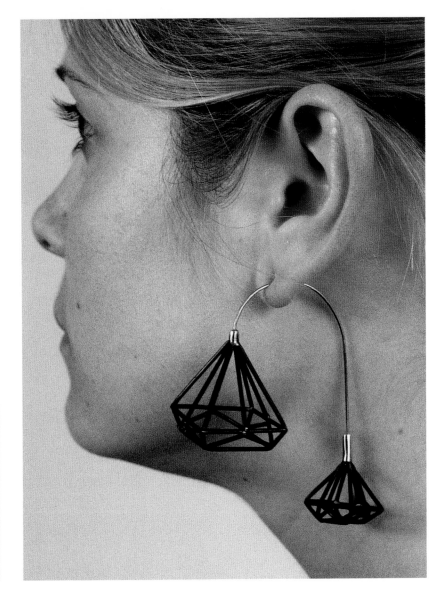

Laura Coddens

Anniversary | 2006

EACH, 6.5 X 2.5 X 4.5 CM

Steel, rubber, sterling silver;
hand fabricated

PHOTOS BY AMY WEIKS

Biba Schutz

Grassy Hoops | 2005

EACH, 3.1 X 2.5 X 3.1 CM

Sterling silver; pierced,
forged, fabricated, oxidized

PHOTO BY RON BOSZKO
COURTESY OF SHERRIE GALLERIE, COLUMBUS, OHIO

Octavia Cook

Cook and Co. Monogram Earrings | 2005

EACH, 10.5 X 1.8 X 0.5 CM

Sterling silver; hand
fabricated, oxidized

PHOTO BY STUDIO LA GONDA

Octavia Cook

Cook and Co. Octopus Earrings | 2005

EACH, 4.2 X 1.8 X 0.8 CM

Sterling silver, cut crystal; hand
fabricated, oxidized

PHOTO BY STUDIO LA GONDA

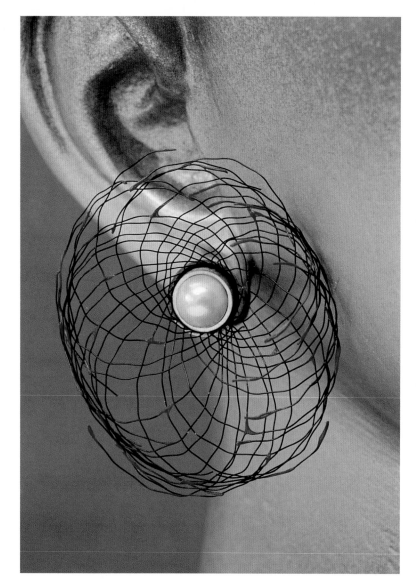

Barbara Cohen

Fireworks | 2006

4 X 4 X 2 CM

Sterling silver, 18-karat gold, cultured pearls,
nylon mesh, rubber; hand fabricated

PHOTO BY ARTIST

Davide Bigazzi
4 Seasons | 2004
EACH, 5 X 2.3 CM
Sterling silver; hand fabricated,
chased, repoussé, oxidized
PHOTO BY ARTIST

Shihoko Amano
Nazuna #1 | 2003
EACH, 7 X 2 X 2 CM
Sterling silver, boxwood,
dye; fabricated
PHOTO BY KEN YANOVIAK

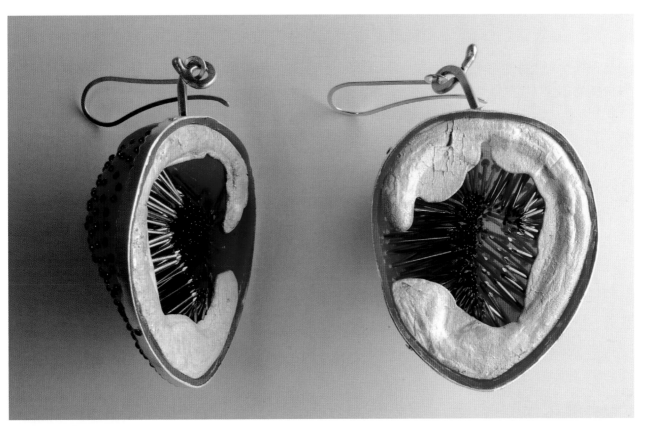

Jenna Wainwright
Untitled | 2006
EACH, 6.7 X 4.6 X 2 CM
Silver, plastic toy, brass
pins; cast, assembled
PHOTOS BY ARTIST

Ellen Himic
Slide and Snap Earrings | 2006
EACH, 7.6 X 2.5 X 2.5 CM
SLA (stereolithography apparatus)
epoxy resin rapid prototyped
PHOTO BY SELECTIVE PHOTOGRAPHY

Hannah Louise Lamb
Oval Wallpaper Cutout Mismatch Earrings | 2006
LEFT, 5 X 3.5 X 0.1 CM
Copper, cold enamel;
hand pierced
PHOTO BY ARTIST

Jennifer W. Chachenian
Untitled | 2005
EACH, 5 X 2.5 X 1 CM
Sterling silver, rubber;
hand fabricated
PHOTO BY MARK JOHNSTON

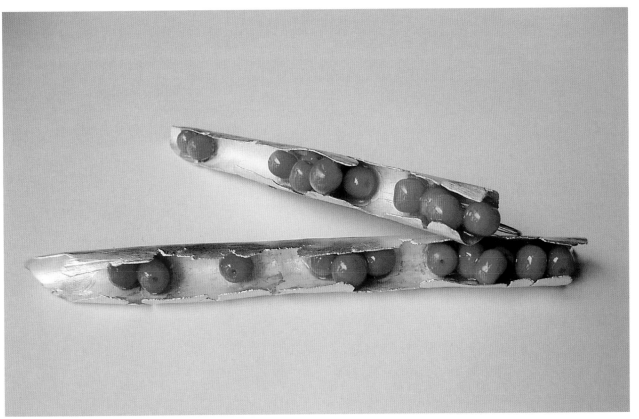

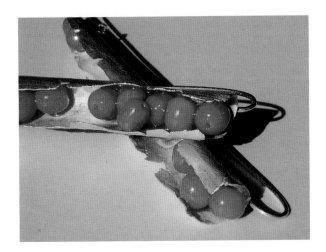

Jenna Wainwright
Untitled | 2006
EACH, 6.7 X 4.6 X 2 CM
Silver, plastic toy, brass
pins; cast, assembled
PHOTOS BY ARTIST

Marjorie Simon
Ear Discs | 2005
EACH, 3.5 CM IN DIAMETER
Copper, enamel;
embossed, kiln fired
PHOTO BY RALPH GABRINER

Marjorie Schick
Spiral Earring for Spira Galaxy | 2002

EARRING, 10.7 X 9.1 X 2.5 CM;
ON STAND, 19.6 X 21.5 X 6.3 CM

Wood, paper-mâché, paint,
wire; constructed

PHOTOS BY GARY POLLMILLER;
MODEL, KATHLENE ALLIE

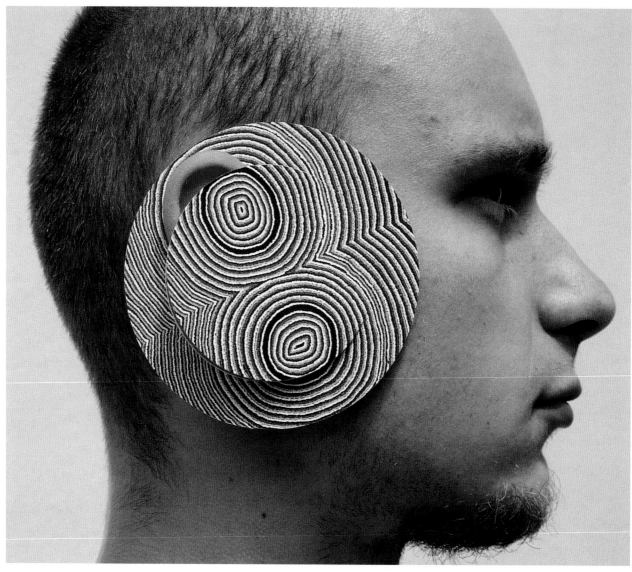

Pavel Herynek

Ear Ornament | 2002
(from the *Ear Ornaments* Series, 2002–2006)
10 CM IN DIAMETER
Cardboard, postcard; cut

PHOTO BY ARTIST

Since 2002, I have been creating an endless series of ornaments made out of postcards, invitation cards, and packaging. I am delighted with the change. The original, informative purpose of an object is altered and—at the same time—enriched with decorative, as well as poetic functions. PAVEL HERYNEK

Sarah Wilbanks
Untitled | 2004
EACH, 6.1 X 1.7 X 0.5 CM
Sterling silver, polymer clay; cast,
hand fabricated, image transfer
PHOTO BY DOUG YAPLE

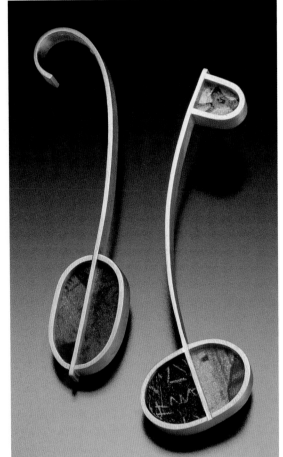

Karen J. Lauseng
The Elegance of Coffee | 2006
EACH, 12.5 X 6.5 X 0.5 CM
Sterling silver, 14-karat gold,
coffee filters; cuttlefish cast
PHOTO BY ARTIST

Alan Revere
Untitled | 1973
9.5 X 4.4 X 1 CM
Sterling silver,
ivory; fabricated
PHOTO BY ARTIST

Julie Jerman-Melka
Gentle Current Earrings | 2005
EACH, 4 X 1.2 X 0.6 CM
Beach pebble, sterling silver, 18-karat
gold, aquamarines; hand carved,
forged, fabricated, tube set
PHOTO BY HAP SAKWA

Hratch Babikian

The Dancers | 2003

EACH, 7.5 X 2 X 1 CM

Ebony, sterling silver, 14-karat gold; fabricated, carved

PHOTO BY ARTIST
COLLECTION OF L. BURNS

Izaskun Zabala
Whispers | 2004
EACH, 11.5 X 11.5 CM
Feathers, silver wire, cotton
cord; hand fabricated

Yuka Saito

Untitled | 2006

13 X 5 X 5 CM

Recycled polypropylene,
polyurethane, sterling silver

PHOTO BY ARTIST

Kiren Niki Sangra
Ear Wings | 2005
EACH, 10 X 7 CM
Silver, aluminum; anodized,
hand fabricated, riveted
PHOTO BY ARTIST

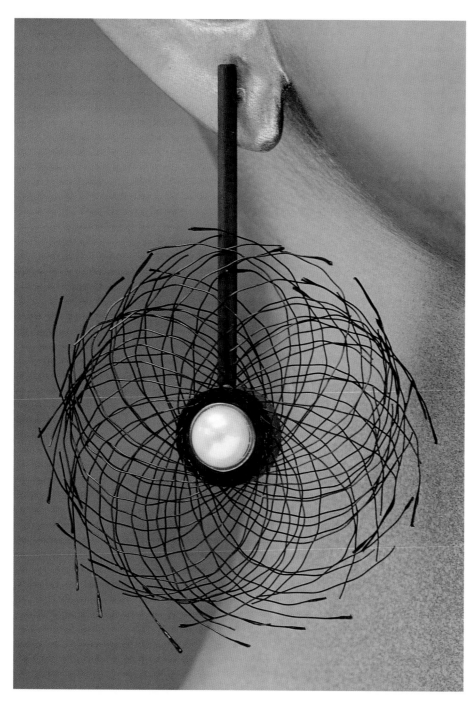

Barbara Cohen
Pinwheel | 2006
7 X 5 X 1.5 CM
Sterling silver, 18-karat
gold, cultured pearls,
nylon mesh, rubber; hand
fabricated, oxidized
PHOTO BY ARTIST

K.C. Calum
Granite Earrings #3 | 2006
EACH, 6 X 4 X 2.5 CM
Wood, rubber, paint
PHOTO BY ARTIST

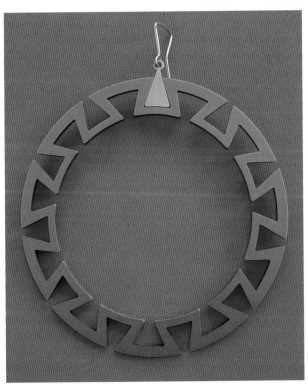

Fritz Maierhofer
Untitled | 2006
9 X 10.5 X 0.3 CM
18-karat gold, aluminum;
oxidized, hand fabricated
PHOTO BY ARTIST

303

Sumner Silverman
Untitled | 2003
EACH, 2 X 2 X 0.5 CM

24-karat gold, 22-karat gold, 18-karat gold, mammoth fossil ivory, ruby, pearl, polymer clay; carved, fabricated

PHOTO BY DEAN POWELL
COURTESY OF SKYLIGHT JEWELERS,
BOSTON, MASSACHUSETTS

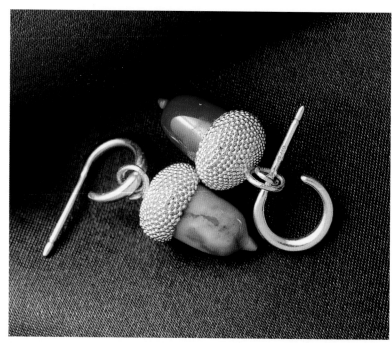

Cecelia Bauer
Acorn Earrings | 2005
EACH, 1.7 X 0.9 X 0.9 CM
22-karat gold, jasper; granulation, hand fabricated, hand cut
PHOTO BY ED ADDEO

Especially with earrings, how they move and fit on the body is very important to us. JEFF WISE AND SUSAN WISE

Jeff Wise and Susan Wise
Soft Geometry #3 | 2002
LONGEST, 6 X 2.5 CM
22-karat gold, 18-karat gold, red coral, moonstone, tourmaline; hand fabricated, articulated, inlay

PHOTO BY PAUL AMBROSE
COURTESY OF AARON FABER GALLERY, NEW YORK, NEW YORK

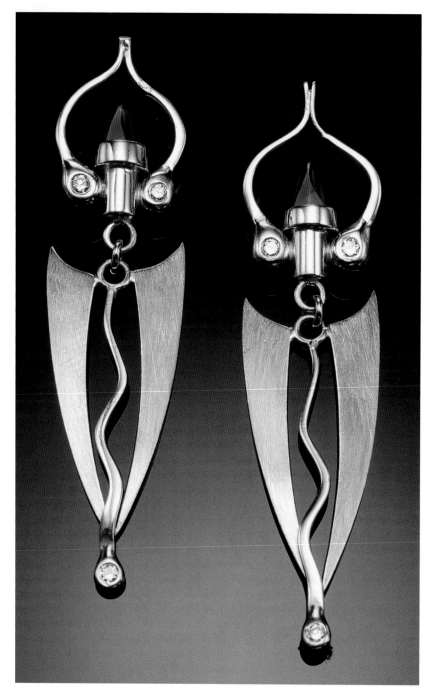

Wayne Werner

Lifedrop II | 2002

EACH, 5 X 1.5 X 0.5 CM

18-karat gold, citrine, diamonds;
hand fabricated, forged

PHOTO BY RALPH GABRINER

Leila Tai

Tiger Lily Earrings | 2005–2006

EACH, 4 X 3 X 0.5 CM

18-karat gold, emerald, pearls;
plique-à-jour, hand fabricated, pierced

PHOTO BY RALPH GABRINER

The pierced gold work, traditionally done by hand, was done through Rhinoceros, a computer program for drawing and modeling shapes. A highly precise drawing is scanned into the program and redrawn as is. One can execute lines as thin as 0.5 mm to allow a model to be made for a limited edition. However, the plique-à-jour process makes each piece unique because it is hard to duplicate the painting technique and the colors. LEILA TAI

Kate Wolf

Acorn Earrings | 1991

EACH, 4.2 X 1.9 X 1.9 CM

18-karat green gold,
rhodolite garnets; hand carved,
cast, hammer set

PHOTO BY KEVIN BRUISIE

Jack Jennings
Untitled | 2002
LEFT, 3.7 X 1.5 CM; RIGHT, 3.5 X 1.4 CM
18-karat gold, 22-karat gold, boulder
opal, garnet; fused, formed, fabricated
PHOTO BY ROBERT DIAMANTE

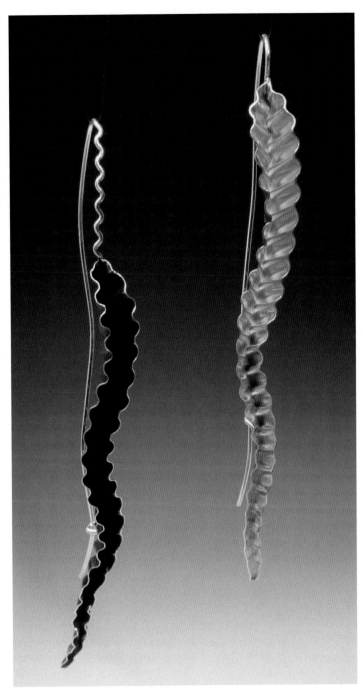

Cynthia Eid

Bee Lines | 2003

EACH, 10 X 0.7 X 0.7 CM

18-karat yellow gold, sterling silver bimetal, sterling silver, patina; micro-folded, fold formed, hand fabricated

PHOTO BY ARTIST
COURTESY OF MOBILIA GALLERY,
CAMBRIDGE, MASSACHUSETTS

Christine Dhein
Untitled | 2005
EACH, 3.5 X 0.5 X 0.5 CM
18-karat yellow gold, rubber, diamonds;
hand fabricated, tube set
PHOTO BY ARTIST

Sasha Samuels
Black and Whites | 1995
EACH, 0.3 X 0.3 X 0.2 CM
22-karat gold, pearls,
garnet; granulation
PHOTO BY DANIEL VAN ROSSEN

Beth Rosengard
Akimbo | 2003
EACH, 4.1 X 1.6 X 0.7 CM
14-karat gold, 18-karat gold, 22-karat
gold, hessonite, coral, rhodolite;
hand fabricated, formed, forged
PHOTO BY ARTIST

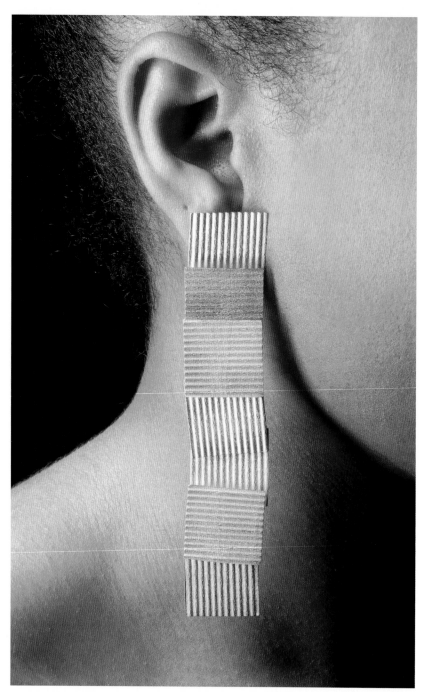

Annamaria Zanella
Skyn | 2005
9 X 2 X 0.4 CM
22-karat gold;
hand fabricated
PHOTO BY GIULIO RUSTICHELLI

Todd Reed
Untitled | 2004
EACH, 2.3 X 2.3 X 0.3 CM
22-karat yellow gold, 18-karat
yellow gold, sterling silver, patina,
raw diamonds, cut diamonds;
hand forged, fabricated
PHOTO BY AZAD

Sarah Graham Metalsmithing
Rattlesnake Grass Earrings | 2006
EACH, 2.3 X 1 CM
Organic rattlesnake grass, 18-karat
yellow gold, steel, diamonds; cast
PHOTO BY HAP SAKWA

Paulette Myers

Voyage | 2004

EACH, 4.4 X 2.2 X 0.7 CM

18-karat yellow gold, bullet-cut
black onyx; reticulated, fabricated

PHOTO BY ARTIST

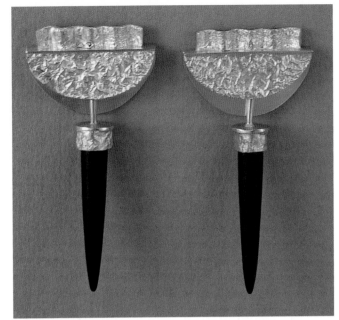

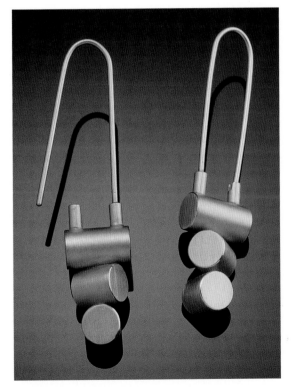

Geoffrey D. Giles

Three Tube | 2006

EACH, 4.8 X 1.3 X 0.6 CM

18-karat yellow gold, 18-karat white
gold; hollow form fabricated, brushed
finish, surface embellished

PHOTO BY TAYLOR DABNEY

Sandy Baker
Sun Dance | 1994
EACH, 7.6 X 1.9 X 0.2 CM
14-karat gold; photoetched,
hand fabricated
PHOTO BY ARTIST

Jonathan Hernandez
BYE-BYE Superman Suite | 2006
EACH, 21 X 18 CM
Brass
PHOTO BY ROBLY GLOVER

Catherine Clark Gilbertson
Spiral Earpiece | 2005
2.6 X 5.7 CM
18-karat gold; chased, repoussé
PHOTOS BY TOM MCINVAILLE

The study and performance of music has paralleled my concentration in visual art throughout my life. This interest has prompted an investigation into the production of music as an organization of pitch waves and the dialogue that exists between the perception and reality of sound. The ear, historically adorned with precious metal, is also the receptor for music. I have undertaken a rhythmic exploration of the ear through chasing and repousse, creating wearable sculpture that is a visualization of the aural experience. CATHERINE CLARK GILBERTSON

Liaung-Chung Yen
Untitled | 2006
EACH, 2 X 2 X 0.8 CM
18-karat gold, diamonds
PHOTO BY ARTIST

Mariel Pagliai
Springtime | 2006
LARGEST, 5 X 3 X 0.3 CM
18-karat gold,
cubic zirconia
PHOTO BY ARTIST

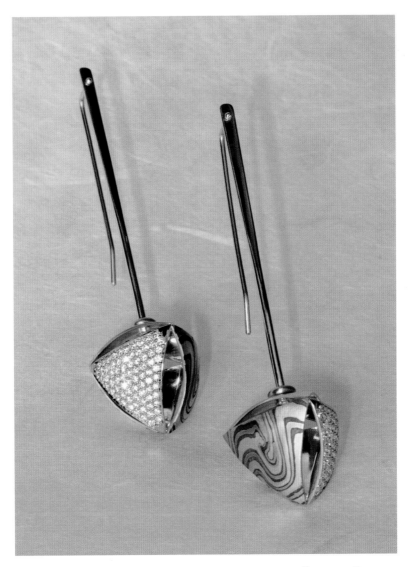

George Sawyer

Mokume Pavé Lantern Earrings | 2006

EACH, 6.5 X 1.8 X 1.8 CM

18-karat gold, copper mokume gane,
diamonds, 18-karat white gold, 22-karat
gold; hand fabricated, pave set

PHOTO BY ARTIST

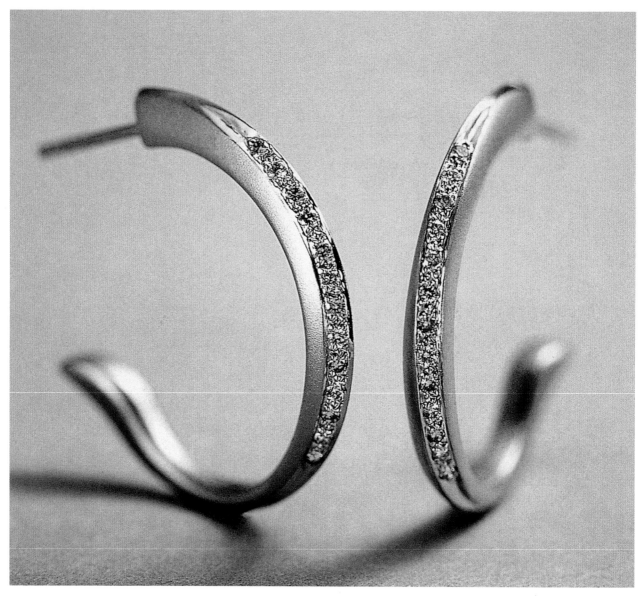

Sasha Samuels

Freedom Hoops | 2001

EACH, 0.3 X 0.3 X 0.8 CM

Platinum, diamonds

PHOTO BY DANIEL VAN ROSSEN

These hoops can be worn with the diamonds facing forward, or they can be reversed to hide the stones. SASHA SAMUELS

Eddie Sakamoto

Rain Showers | 2005

EACH, 3.5 X 1.1 X 0.3 CM

18-karat gold, diamonds;
cast, hand fabricated

PHOTO BY ARTIST

Mia Maljojoki
Jellyfish | 2003
EACH, 9 X 5 X 5 CM
18-karat gold, silver, pearl, plastic
PHOTO BY DEAN POWELL

In my process of researching the various forms linking culture and identity, my work continues to intermediate between the abused and the cherished, the valued and the abandoned. Curiosities intends to be a collection of absurd odditities emblematic of the things that are hidden under the rocks and under the bed. It is an outwardly reflective process, moving in the peripheral spaces of the wasteland and overturning what we have discarded. In an effort to recreate the unimaginably repressed, waste plastic is reinvigorated with personal meaning; and thus, it is shown that value and worth are inextricably linked to the the unwanted and the coveted. Bridget Catchpole

Bridget Catchpole
Curiosities Series | 2006
EACH, 3.8 X 1.6 CM
Sterling silver, thermoplastic, rubber; hand fabricated, molded
PHOTO BY ANTHONY MCLEAN

Mia Maljojoki
Flora #1 | 2003
EACH, 6 X 8 X 6 CM
18-karat gold, fish scales, plastic

PHOTO BY CARY WOLINSKY
COURTESY OF MOBILIA GALLERY,
CAMBRIDGE, MASSACHUSETTS

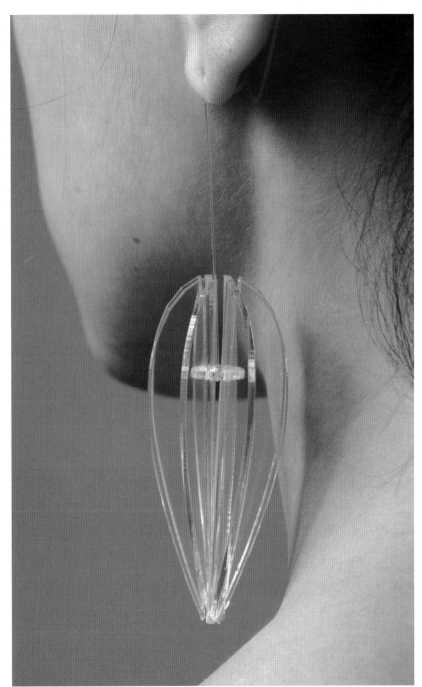

Laura Aragon
Clarion | 2006
4.4 X 3.2 X 3.2 CM
Acrylic, monofilament;
laser cut
PHOTO BY MICHAEL O'NEILL

Nadia Morgenthaler Dupont
Lanterne Orientale | 2004
EACH, 6 X 2.5 X 2.5 CM
Sterling silver, pearl; hand fabricated
PHOTO BY ANDRÉ DUPONT

Patricia Zabreski Venaleck
Dotted Swiss Wings | 2006
EACH, 2.5 X 0.8 X 0.5 CM
Glass, sterling silver; lampworked,
forged, soldered
PHOTO BY JERRY ANTHONY

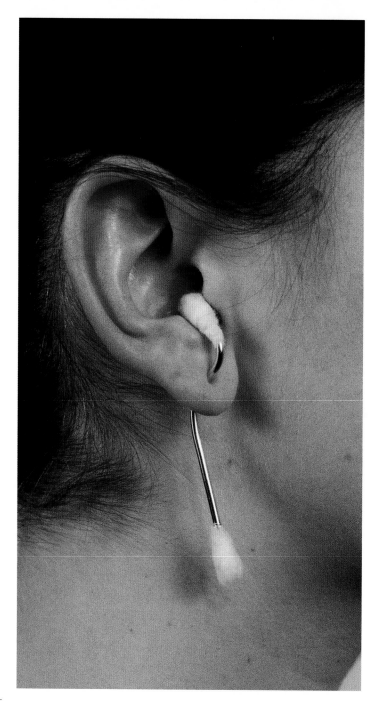

Jackie Juhasz
Untitled | 2006
EACH, 6 X 2 X 1 CM
Sterling silver, cotton; hand
fabricated, tap and dye
PHOTOS BY AMY WEIKS

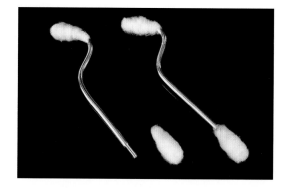

Elizabeth Ann Tokoly
Orchids | 1994
EACH, 3.8 X 1.9 X 7.6 CM
Sterling silver, garnet, stainless steel
PHOTO BY ARTIST

I have been examining geometry in nature. Geometry is a branch of mathematics that deals with the relationship of points, lines, angles, surfaces, and solids. Geometry is the configuration or arrangement of parts. Nature is complex, yet simple, simultaneously. Nature and geometry are ultimate order; however, nature presents deviation and disorder. Geometry gives the artist precision and nature provides abundance.

ELIZABETH ANN TOKOLY

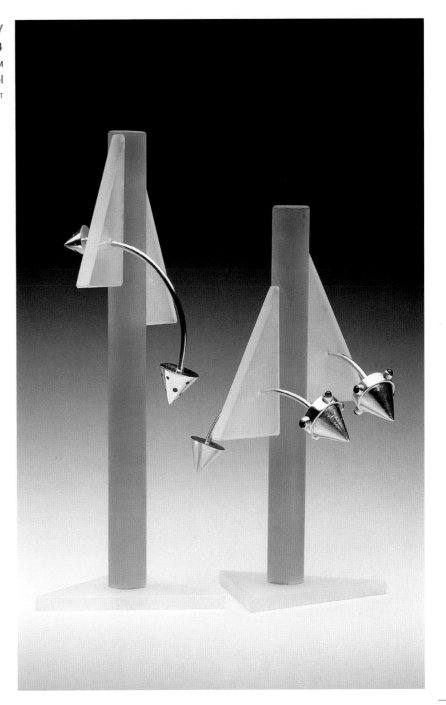

K.C. Calum

Earrings | 2006

EACH, 12.5 X 12.5 X 3 CM

Wood, rubber, paint

PHOTO BY ARTIST

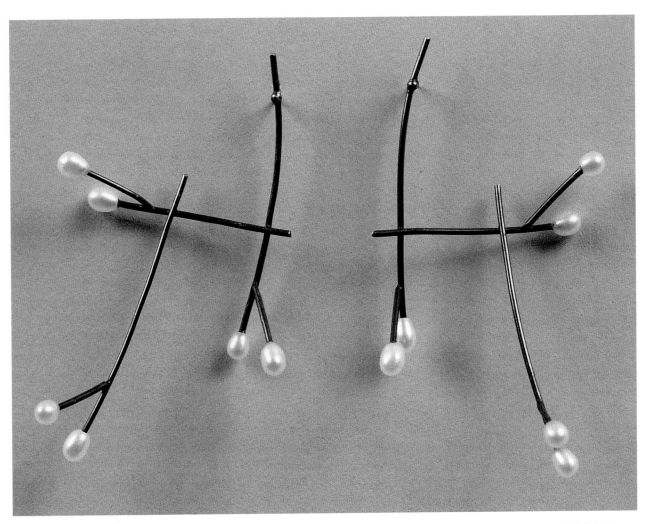

Micki Lippe
Twig Earrings | 2006
EACH, 5 X 5 X 1 CM
Sterling silver, pearls; hand
fabricated, oxidized
PHOTO BY RICHARD NICOL

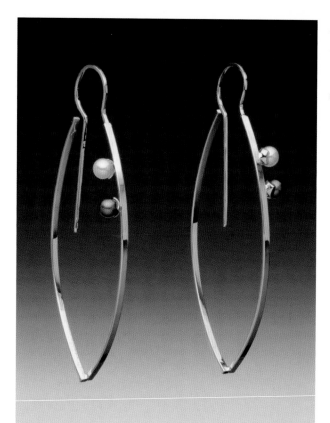

Amy Burkholder
Balance | 2006
EACH, 6.4 X 2.6 X 0.5 CM
18-karat yellow gold, pearls
PHOTO BY GEORGE POST

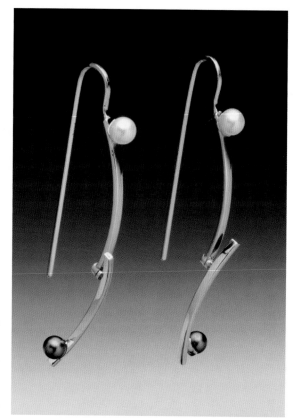

Amy Burkholder
Moon Dance | 2006
EACH, 5.1 X 1.9 X 0.5 CM
18-karat yellow gold,
pearls; riveted
PHOTO BY GEORGE POST

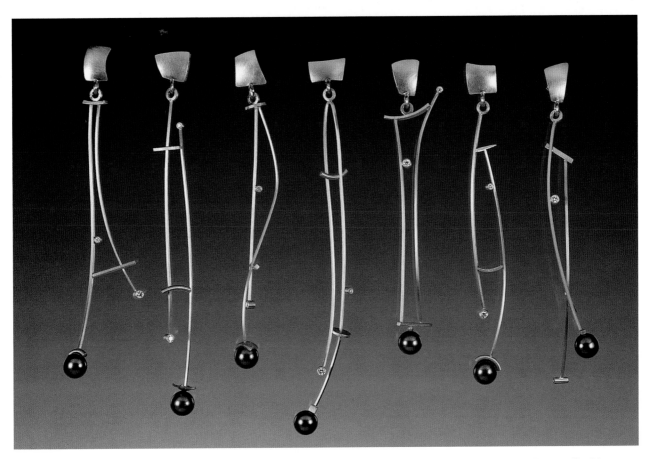

After doing many pairs of mismatched earrings, I thought the next logical step was to do a whole series that could be mixed and matched. No two earrings are perfectly matched, but any two can be worn together. BRENT R. KEENEY

Brent R. Keeney
7 and 7 Is...
Seven Unmatched
Ear Ornaments | 2006
LONGEST, 10 X 1.2 X 1 CM
14-karat white gold, 18-karat
yellow gold, diamonds, pearls;
hand fabricated

PHOTO BY ARTIST

Loretta Fontaine

Pinnate Series—Earrings #2 | 1998

EACH, 5 X 2 X 0.5 CM

Sterling silver, freshwater
pearls, polymer clay; nerikomi,
hand fabricated

PHOTO BY ARTIST

Karen J. Lauseng
Untitled | 2006

EACH, 9.5 X 1.8 X 0.5 CM

Sterling silver, pearls, quilling
paper, 14-karat gold; woven

PHOTO BY ARTIST

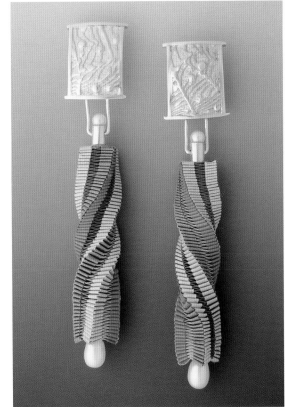

Dolores Barrett

Ellipses Earrings | 2006

EACH, 4.5 X 1.2 X 1.2 CM

Dichroic and art glass, gold-filled
wire; fused, hand polished

PHOTO BY ARTIST

Yoshie Hattori
Coral Earrings | 2006

7 X 3 X 3 CM

Steel thread, red coral,
silver; knitted

PHOTO BY BRAD MCPHEE
COLLECTION OF STEVEN FORTH

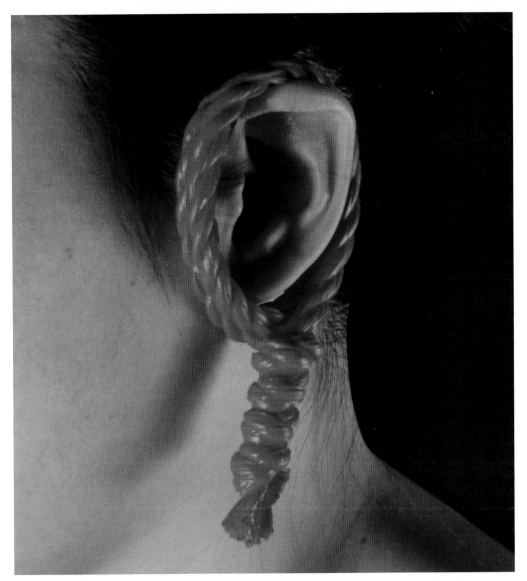

Sungyeoul Lee
Knot So Precious | 2006
12 X 5.6 X 1.6 CM
Poly rope, flexible rubber
coating; hand fabricated
PHOTO BY ARTIST

Dee Fontans
Untitled | 2001
9 X 5 X 0.5 CM
Sterling silver, steel, paint
PHOTO BY CHARLES LEWTON-BRAIN

The earring is a visual representation of sound. DEE FONTANS

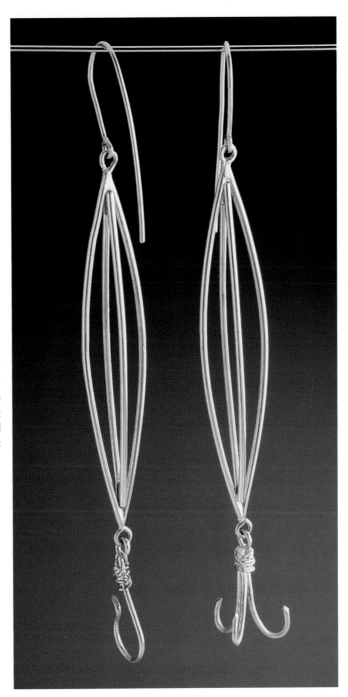

Lulu Lederman
Fishing Lure Earrings | 2004
EACH, 8 X 1.2 X 1.2 CM
14-karat gold, sterling silver;
hand drawn, fabricated
PHOTO BY MARTY DOYLE

Cheryl Sills
Untitled | 2006
EACH, 1.5 X 1 X 0.5 CM
Silver, rubber stones; cast
PHOTO BY STUDIO LA GONDA

Tiffany Brotherton
Interchangable Earrings | 2005
EACH, 10 X 6 X 6 CM
Sterling silver, 18-karat gold;
planished, hand fabricated
PHOTO BY SARAH PERKINS

Hsiao Chia-Pei
Listens to the Sea | 2006
10 X 8 X 2 CM
Plastic; sawed
PHOTO BY ARTIST

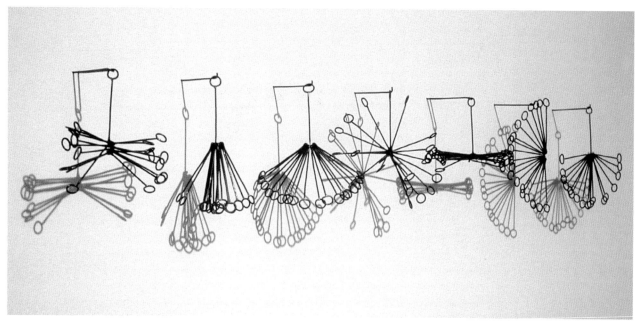

Kristine Bolhuis

Seven Iterations of an Earring | 2003

EACH, 8 X 8 X 8 CM

Steel, sterling silver;
hand fabricated

PHOTOS BY ARTIST

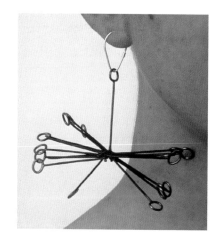

Daphne Krinos
Untitled | 2006
EACH, 5.2 X 2 X 0.5 CM
Silver, rutilated quartz,
diamonds; oxidized
PHOTO BY JOËL DEGEN

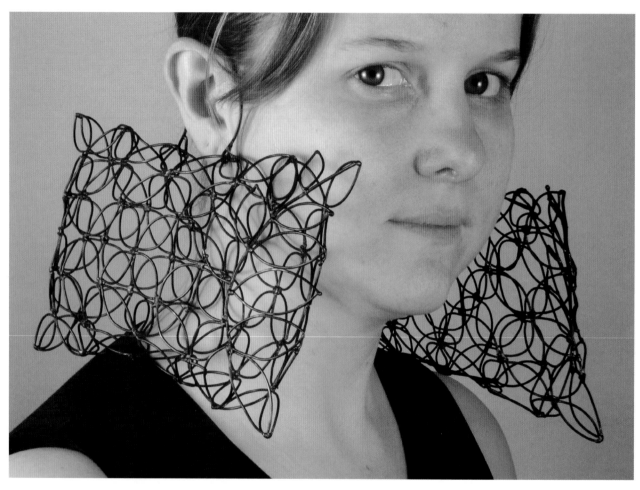

Megan Auman
Pillow Earrings | 2005
EACH, 21.6 X 10.2 X 5.1 CM
Steel; welded
PHOTO BY ARTIST

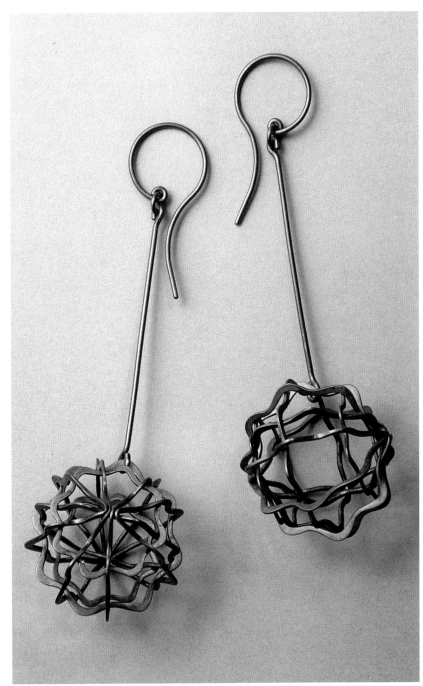

Kirsten Clausager
Flora Con Amore #3 | 2006
EACH, 9 X 3 X 3 CM
Sterling silver; oxidized, hand
fabricated, bent, soldered, rolled
PHOTO BY OLE AKHOJ

Lisa Crowder

The Swans | 2005

EACH, 10.2 X 6.4 X 5.1 CM

Sterling silver; hand fabricated,
pierced, soldered, formed, oxidized

PHOTO BY HAP SAKWA

Eun Mi Kim
Sorting II | 2003
LONGEST, 13 X 4 X 4 CM
Sterling silver, nylon, 24-karat
gold; hand fabricated, raised,
soldered, kum boo, oxidized
PHOTOS BY PETER NASSOIT

Kathryn Yeats
Untitled | 2006
LEFT, 5 X 1.5 X 2 CM;
RIGHT, 2.2 X 2.7 X 2 CM
Sterling silver, patina; hand
fabricated, oxidized
PHOTO BY ARTIST

Miriam Verbeek
There Was a Little Boy | 1998
8 X 2.5 X 0.8 CM
Silver, slide, resin
PHOTO BY HENNIE VAN BEEK

*I made these earrings after the death of a little boy. The hummingbird, a
symbol of death and passion, carries the swing in his bill. There is nobody
sitting on the swing. Only his eyes rock slowly when you wear these earrings.
This piece is from a series of mourning jewelry.* MIRIAM VERBEEK

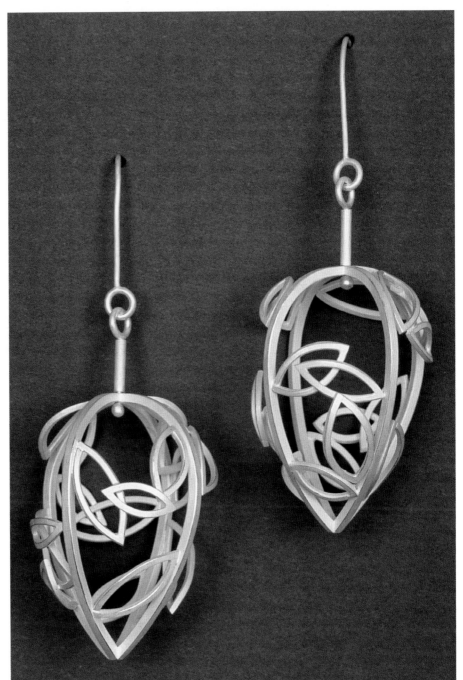

Hyejeong Ko
Earrings | 2002
EACH, 8 X 3.5 X 3.5 CM
Sterling silver; hand fabricated
PHOTO BY DAN NEUBERGER

Kerstin Nichols
Pod Earrings | 2005
EACH, 5.5 X 1.8 X 1.5 CM
Sterling silver; hand fabricated,
roller printed, stamped, oxidized
PHOTO BY ARTIST

These elegant, plant inspired, modern earrings dangle and sway when worn. GLEN ESK

Glen Esk

Phlox Long Stem Earrings | 2001
EACH, 7.7 X 1.7 X 1.2 CM
Silver; hand fabricated, formed,
soldered, oxidized
PHOTO BY SUZANNE POTTER

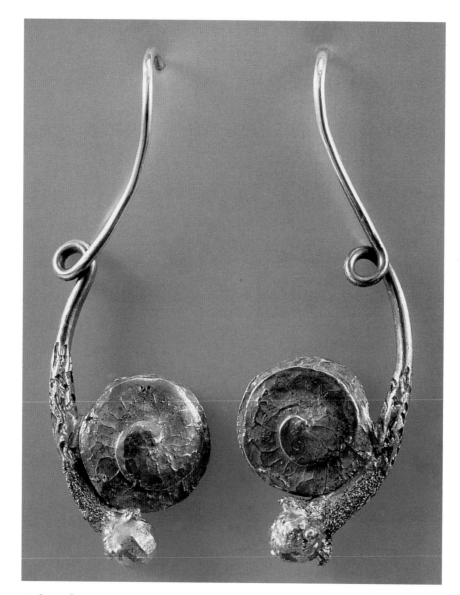

Rob Jackson

Snail | 2001

EACH, 3.5 X 1.3 X 0.6 CM

Silver, 18-karat gold, seed pods, clove
spice; cast, hand fabricated, forged

PHOTO BY ARTIST

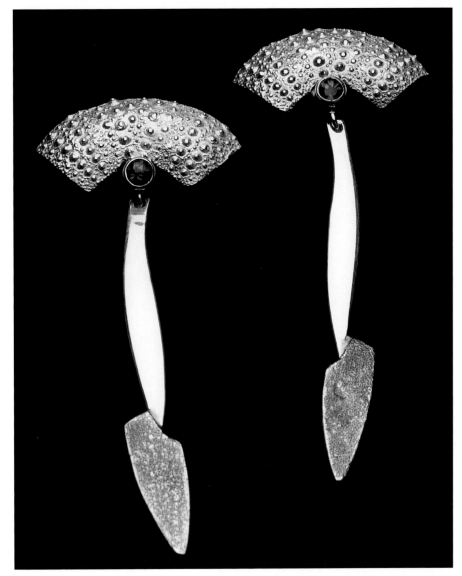

Hratch Babikian

Sea Weed Dangle | 2005

EACH, 6 X 1 X 0.5 CM

Sterling silver, 14-karat gold, garnet;
fabricated, forged, cast, buffed, textured

PHOTO BY ARTIST

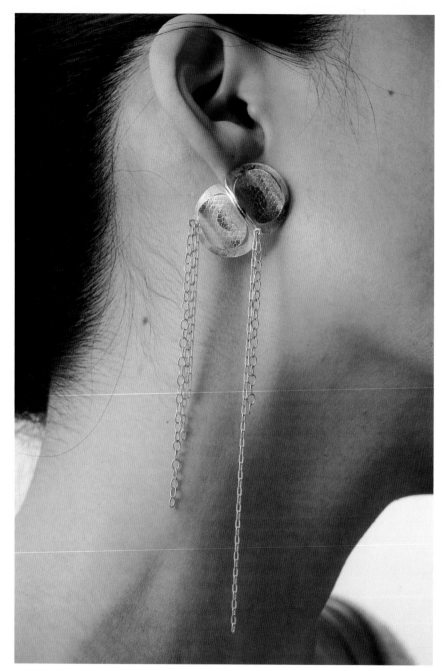

Jennifer Yi

Untitled | 2006

12 X 2.5 X 2 CM

24-karat gold, sterling silver; hand fabricated, roller printed, kum boo

PHOTO BY NICK PARISSE

Neda Nassiri
Untitled | 2006
EACH, 4.2 X 0.4 X 0.4 CM
18-karat gold, fine silver;
hand fabricated
PHOTOS BY ILEEN KOHN SOSA

Lee Ramsey Haga
Lightning Over River | 2003
EACH, 3.7 X 1.7 X 0.5 CM
Shibuishi, sterling silver, 23-karat gold leaf,
variscite, patina; reticulated, hand fabricated
PHOTO BY PAUL YONCHEK
COURTESY OF CONTEMPORARY CRAFTS MUSEUM
AND GALLERY, PORTLAND, OREGON

David Bausman

Porcupine Quill Talisman | 2006

45 X 7 X 3 CM

Sterling silver, porcupine
quills; die formed, fabricated

PHOTO BY ARTIST

Cathy Chotard
Untitled | 2006
EACH, 5 X 0.4 X 0.4 CM
Sterling silver, nylon thread
PHOTO BY ARTIST

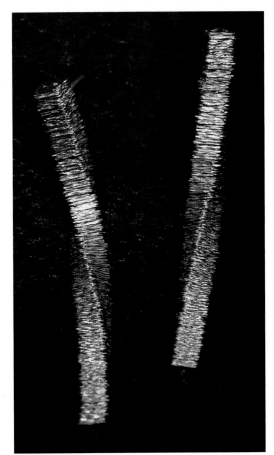

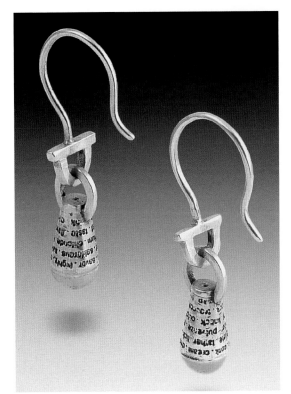

Douglas Close
Untitled | 2005
EACH, 3.8 X 0.7 X 0.7 CM
Silver, bronze; etched,
hand fabricated
PHOTO BY BARRY BLAU PHOTOGRAPHY

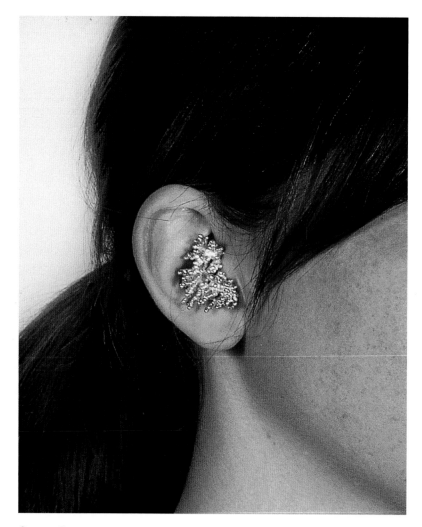

Stacy Petersen
Coral Earpiece | 2005
2 X 3 X 2 CM
Sterling silver; cast
PHOTO BY ARTIST

Amy Cannon
Seed Bunches | 2000
EACH, 5.7 X 3.2 X 2.5 CM
Sterling silver; hand fabricated,
matte finished, oxidized
PHOTO BY RICHARD WALKER

Amy Cannon
Double Daisies | 2005
EACH, 4.5 X 2.5 X 1.3 CM
Sterling silver, 18-karat gold, Mexican
fire opal; hand fabricated, polished
PHOTO BY RICHARD WALKER

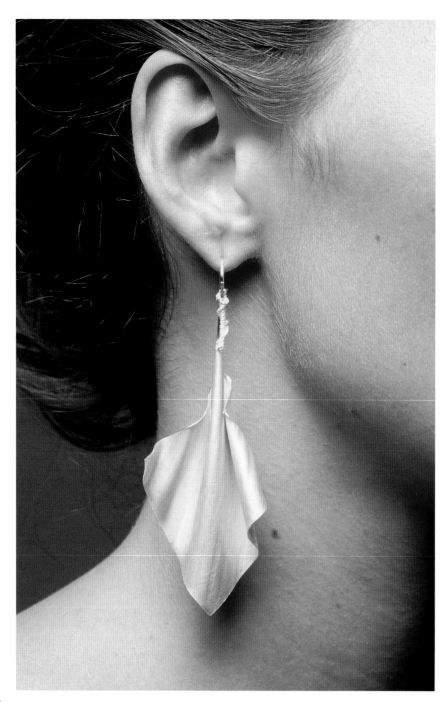

Bronwyn Jayne Pressey
Silk Crinkle | 2006
8.5 X 3.5 X 1.2 CM
Fine silver, sterling silver, knotted
silk thread; roller printed
PHOTO BY THERESE DE VILLIERS

Chih-Wen Chiu
Variety | 2004
EACH, 7.3 X 2.6 X 2.3 CM
Sterling silver; hand
fabricated, linked
PHOTO BY DAN NEUBURGER

Nadia Morgenthaler Dupont
L'Aulne Châtons | 1997
EACH, 6 X 0.7 X 0.7 CM
Sterling silver, fishing
line; hand fabricated
PHOTO BY ANDRÉ DUPONT

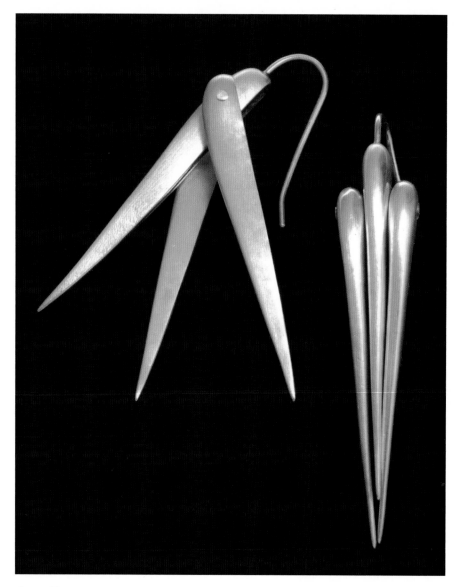

Amy Cannon
Triple Points | 2003
EACH, 4.5 X 0.8 X 0.4 CM
Sterling silver; riveted,
matte finished, oxidized
PHOTO BY RICHARD WALKER

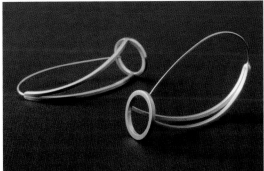

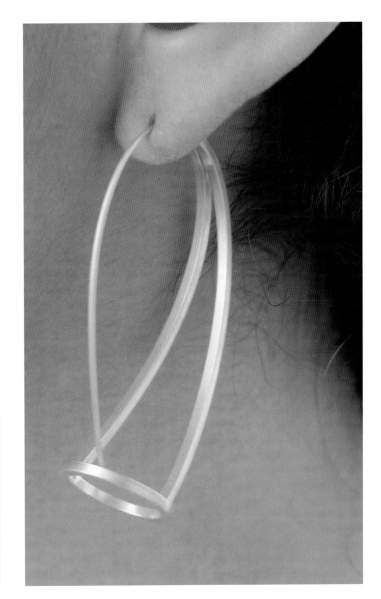

Cheryleve Acosta

Conical Swirl 1 | 2006

EACH, 4.5 X 3.3 X 1.7 CM

Sterling silver;
hand fabricated

PHOTOS BY MICHAEL O'NEILL

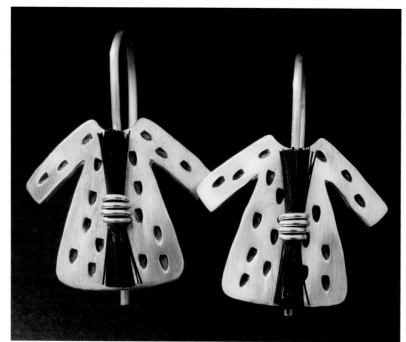

Heidi BigKnife
Untitled, from the
Genetic Memory series | 2006
EACH, 3.5 X 2.5 X 0.6 CM
Sterling silver, horsehair, patina;
hand fabricated, stamped, soldered
PHOTO BY MARK LAPLANTE

Hadar Jacobson
Good Night Moon | 2006
EACH, 3 X 2 CM
Metal clay, moonstone; hand
fabricated, fired, soldered, oxidized
PHOTO BY ARTIST

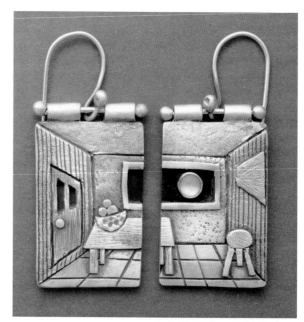

Betty McKim

Earrings | 2005

EACH, 7 CM

Sterling silver; embossed,
hollow formed, oxidized

PHOTO BY ROBERT DIAMANTE

Ann Parkin

Bubble Chamber Window #2 | 1993

EACH, 2.5 X 2.5 CM

Sterling silver; roller printed,
fused, hand fabricated

PHOTO BY RALPH GABRINER

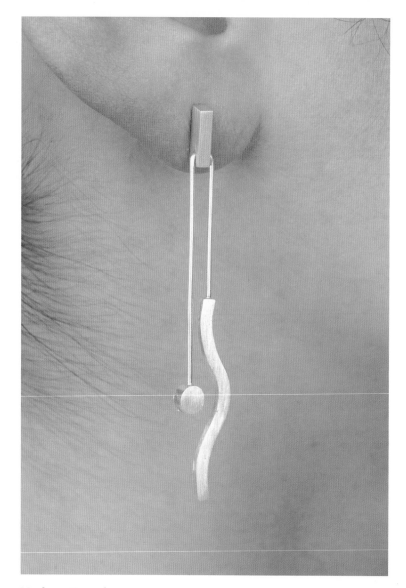

Vasken Tanielian
Untitled | 2006
5.5 X 1 X 0.5 CM
Sterling silver;
fabricated
PHOTO BY CHRISTINE DHEIN

Bruce Anderson
E 88-3 | 1983
EACH, 4.5 X 2.5 X 0.6 CM
18-karat gold, sterling silver,
lapis lazuli, sapphire
PHOTO BY RALPH GABRINER

Charmaine Ho
Empyrean 12 | 2006
EACH, 6.5 X 2 X 0.8 CM
Sterling silver;
hand fabricated
PHOTO BY GEORGE POST

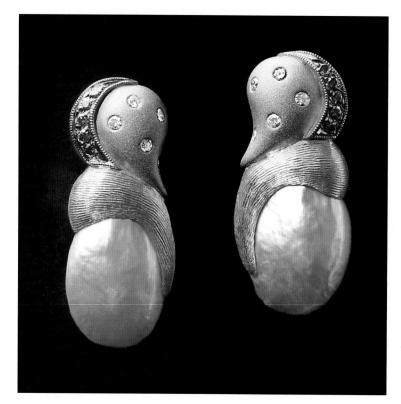

W. Taft Atkins

A Gift to the Queen | 2001

EACH, 4.5 X 2 X 0.5 CM

18-karat green gold, cultured pearls,
diamond brilliants; cast, textured

PHOTO BY ARTIST

Marjorie Simon
Golden Hut Earrings | 2005
EACH, 5 X 1.5 X 0.5 CM
18-karat gold, 14-karat gold,
freshwater pearls; fabricated
PHOTO BY RALPH GABRINER

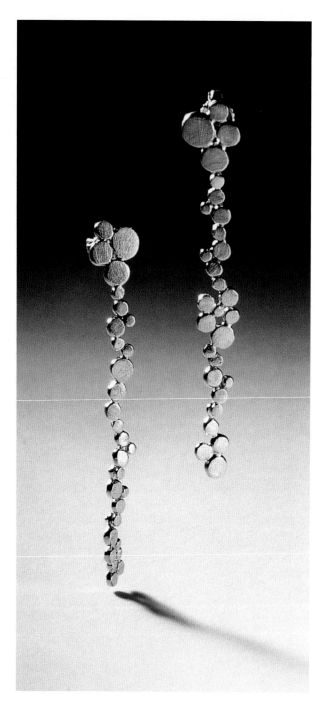

Nina Basharova
Milky Way Drops | 2005
EACH, 6 X 1 X 1 CM
18-karat gold
PHOTO BY CHRISTINA HOLMES

Wayne Werner

Conception Earring | 2005

EACH, 6 X 2 X 0.1 CM

18-karat gold, platinum, black pearl,
diamonds; forged, hinged, flush set

PHOTO BY RALPH GABRINER

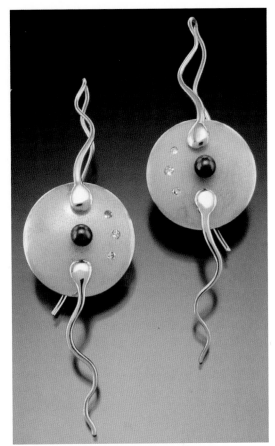

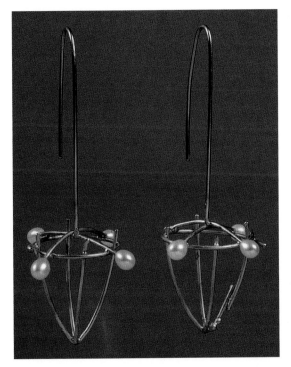

Micki Lippe

Untitled | 2006

EACH, 5 X 1 X 0.1 CM

18-karat gold, pearls;
hand fabricated

PHOTO BY RICHARD NICOL

Thomas Herman

Laurel Leaf Hoops with Black Tahitians | 2006

EACH, 2.7 X 1.3 X 1.3 CM

18-karat white gold, diamonds, pearls;
carved, chased, pierced, inlay

PHOTO BY RALPH GABRINER

Nanz Aalund

Maltese Cross with Tahitian Pearls | 2002

EACH, 2.5 X 0.9 X 0.9 CM

Platinum, pink sapphires,
pearls; hand fabricated

PHOTO BY JIM FORBES

James Kaya
Edge | 2005
EACH, 6.1 CM LONG
Platinum, pearls, diamonds;
hand fabricated
PHOTO BY ROBERT DIAMANTE

Bettina Speckner
Untitled | 2005
EACH, 4.5 X 3 CM
Zinc, silver, diamonds;
photoetched
PHOTO BY ARTIST

Azza Al Qubaisi
Life | 2005
EACH, 2.2 X 0.6 CM
18-karat white gold, diamond;
hand fabricated, hammered
PHOTO BY ARTIST

Paula Crespo
Untitled | 2006
12 X 6.5 CM
Sterling silver; hand
fabricated, oxidized
PHOTO BY CATARINA CRESPO

Delane Cooper

Light on Tine | 2005

EACH, 4.6 X 2.6 X 0.1 CM

14-karat gold, pearls;
hand fabricated

PHOTO BY TRACY CLARE

Anna Heindl
Cherry Blossoms | 2006
EACH, 3 X 2 X 2.2 CM
14-karat red gold, pearls
PHOTO BY MAUFRED WAKOLBIUGER

Carolyn Bensinger
Last Leaf, First Snow | 2005
EACH, 7 X 4 X 0.5 CM
Sterling silver, 18-karat gold, shakudo,
phantom jasper; formed, fabricated, oxidized
PHOTO BY DEAN POWELL

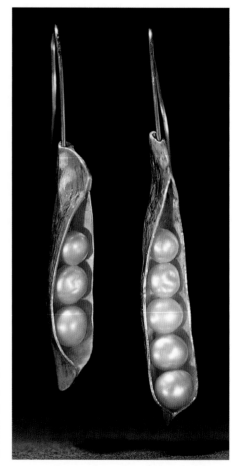

Sarabeth Carnat
Pink Pearl Pea Pods | 1986
EACH, 8.3 X 0.7 X 0.7 CM
18-karat gold, pearls;
constructed
PHOTO BY CHARLES LEWTON-BRAIN

Tricia Lachowiec
Trying to Thrive | 2005
EACH, 4.4 X 2.5 X 1.6 CM
14-karat gold, sterling
silver; fabricated
PHOTO BY DEAN POWELL

Stacy Petersen

Branches | 2006

EACH, 45 X 16 X 5 CM

Found materials, sterling silver

PHOTO BY ARTIST

Josée Desjardins
Drifting I | 2006
EACH, 4.5 X 4.5 X 1.6 CM
Sterling silver, driftwood;
hand fabricated

PHOTO BY ANTHONY MCLEAN
COURTESY OF GALERIE NOËL GUYOMARCH,
MONTREAL, CANADA

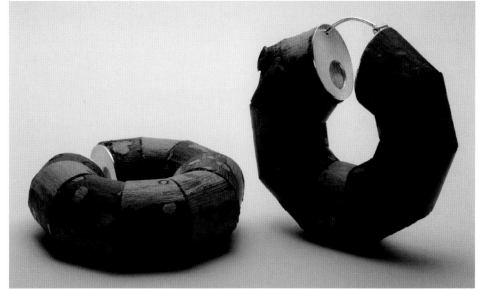

Laurie Dansereau
Fairy-Like Earrings | 2005
EACH, 5 X 3 X 1 CM
Cocobolo, sterling silver;
sculpted, hand fabricated

PHOTO BY ANTHONY MCLEAN

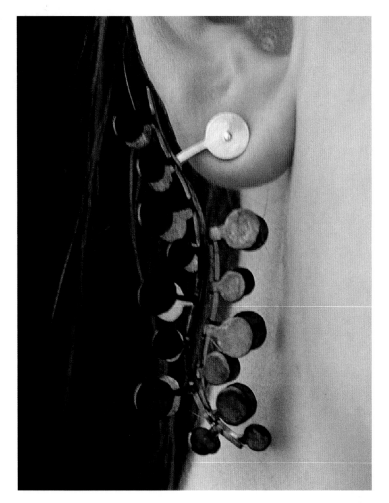

Florencia Gargiulo
Otonal | 2006
5.5 X 2.5 X 2 CM
18-karat gold, shakudo;
hand fabricated, oxidized
PHOTOS BY ARTIST

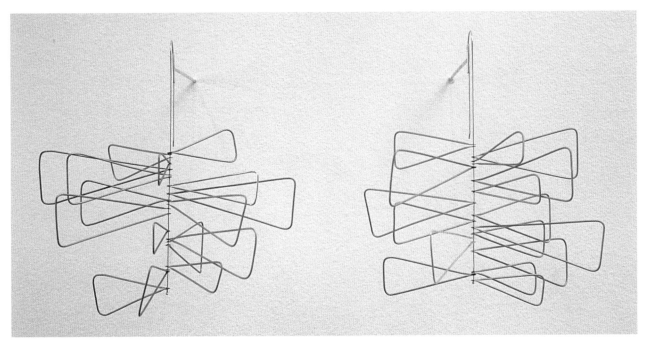

My work evolves at the bench where I explore structual forms using simple hand tools. My recent work has focused on lightweight metal constructions that move, flex, and collapse. I hope that the wearer is encouraged to explore and discover the mobility in this jewelry—a movement that reflects both the motion of the wearer and the inevitable pull of gravity. KRISTINE BOLHUIS

Kristine Bolhuis
Whorl-Triangles | 2003
EACH, 11 X 11 X 11 CM
Titanium, 18-karat gold; hand fabricated with rotating parts
PHOTO BY JOHN GUILLEMIN

Peg Fetter
Untitled | 2004
EACH, 3.5 X 1.5 X 1.5 CM
14-karat gold, prehistoric shark
teeth, diamonds; fabricated, tube set
PHOTO BY DON CASPER

*The dicotomy of two prehistoric elements—
the shark's teeth against the elegance of the
diamond—is especially pleasing.* PEG FETTER

Kenneth MacBain
Untitled | 2006
EACH, 6 X 5 X 0.5 CM
Steel nail, brass, mink fur;
forged, textured, oxidized
PHOTO BY ARTIST

Polly Daeger
Untitled | 2006
EACH, 7.5 X 1.5 X 1.5 CM

Sterling silver, freshwater pearl, patina;
corrugated, fold formed, oxidized

PHOTO BY LARRY SANDERS

Azza Al Qubaisi
Bareeq Al Oudh | 2006
EACH, 3 X 1.2 X 1.2 CM

18-karat yellow gold, agrawood,
idolite; hand fabricated

PHOTO BY ARTIST

In Arabian tradition, using Agrawood (Oudh) was fundamental to everyday life. The curvy shapes, the color of each piece, and the smell makes it unique. A childhood dream came true by capturing the essence of Agrawood in my jewelry collection. AZZA AL QUBAISI

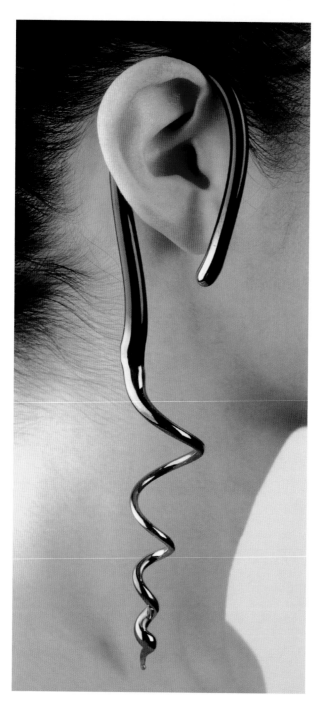

Dustin Revere
Untitled | 2006
17.5 X 0.5 X 4 CM
Blown glass, 24-karat gold
PHOTO BY CHRISTINE DHEIN

Laura Lubin

Cone Earrings | 2006

EACH, 3.6 X 1.7 CM

Soda lime glass, sterling silver; hand
fabricated, lampworked, etched

PHOTO BY PAUL AVIS

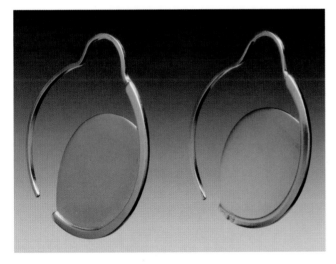

Amy Burkholder

Harvest Moon | 2006

EACH, 3.2 X 3.2 X 0.5 CM

14-karat red gold

PHOTO BY GEORGE POST

Jeff Wise and Susan Wise

Fred and Ginger | 2001

EACH, 6 X 2.5 CM

22-karat gold, 18-karat gold, red coral, black jade,
pearl, mother-of-pearl, garnet; hand fabricated,
articulated movement, carved, inlay

PHOTO BY PAUL AMBROSE
COURTESY OF PATINA GALLERY, SANTA FE, NEW MEXICO

Carolyn Bensinger
Untitled | 2006
EACH, 4.8 X 0.5 X 0.5 CM
18-karat gold, 14-karat gold,
diamonds, found metal; fabricated
PHOTO BY DEAN POWELL

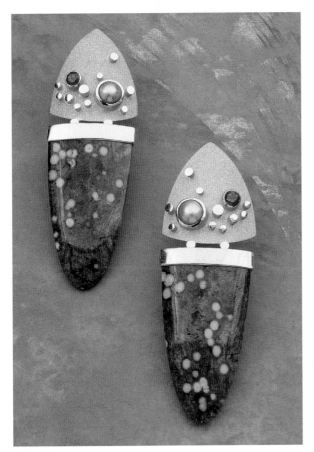

Jeffrey Kaphan
Earrings | 1995
EACH, 6 X 2 CM
14-karat yellow gold, 14-karat white gold,
poppy jasper, pearls, fire opal; fabricated
PHOTO BY PERRY JOHNSON/IMAGICA

Gina Pankowski
Untitled | 1998–2006
EACH, 3.2 CM LONG
Sterling silver, 14-karat
gold, carnelian, patina
PHOTO BY DOUG YAPLE

*My earring designs often
begin as studies for larger
pieces of jewelry. After sketching
patterns, I create three-dimen-
sional models to test how the
links move together. These models
stimulate a never-ending play of
pattern, form, and movement
that is key to my designing
process.* GINA PANKOWSKI

Jill Newbrook

Untitled | 2005

EACH, 5.5 X 1 X 0.7 CM

18-karat white gold,
silver, garnets

PHOTO BY JÖEL DEGEN

Dahlia Kanner

Open Pocket Ears | 1999

EACH, 4 X 2.4 X 0.6 CM

Sterling silver, silver, pearls,
garnet, patina; cast

PHOTO BY MARK JOHNSTON

Kathryn Osgood
Red Flower Earrings | 2006
EACH, 6.5 X 2 X 2 CM
Sterling silver, copper, enamel,
garnet; fabricated
PHOTO BY ROBERT DIAMANTE

Barbara Minor and Christopher A. Hentz
Cable Marquis Earrings | 2001

EACH, 4.4 X 2 X 0.5 CM

Enamel, 24-karat gold foil, formed copper, 22-karat yellow gold

PHOTO BY RALPH GABRINER

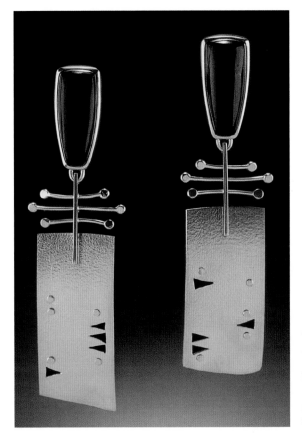

Tami Dean
Untitled | 1992

EACH, 5.7 X 1.9 CM

18-karat gold, 14-karat gold, lapis lazuli; roller printed, pierced, soldered

PHOTO BY RALPH GABRINER

Ronda Coryell
Untitled | 2006
4 X 2.8 CM
22-karat gold, amethyst;
chased, repoussé, granulation
PHOTO BY CHRISTINE DHEIN

Christoph Freier
Fabulous Beasts | 2005
18-karat gold
PHOTO BY ARTIST

Bettina Hübner
1001 Nights | 1995
EACH, 8.2 X 4.4 X 0.3 CM
18-karat yellow gold; cast
PHOTO BY ARTIST

Paul Leathers
Untitled | 1994
EACH, 2.2 X 1.8 X 0.9 CM
14-karat yellow gold, rhodolite
garnets; cast, constructed
PHOTO BY ARTIST

Jeff Wise and Susan Wise

Neptune | 1998

EACH, 5 X 2 CM

18-karat gold, lapis lazuli, turquoise, opal, tanzanite, tourmaline; hand fabricated, inlay, articulated

PHOTO BY PAUL AMBROSE
COURTESY OF CONCEPTS, CARMEL, CALIFORNIA

Glenda Ruth

Morning Vine | 2005

EACH, 7.5 X 1.6 X 0.5 CM

22-karat gold, opal; hand
formed, fused, granulation

PHOTOS BY CHRISTINE DHEIN

Vina Rust

Earrings #10: Stamen Series | 2006

EACH, 4.2 X 3.1 X 0.3 CM

Sterling silver, 22-karat gold, 14-karat
gold, patina; hand fabricated, oxidized

PHOTO BY DOUG YAPLE

Reiko Ishiyama

Earrings II | 2003

EACH, 3.8 X 4.7 X 7 CM

Sterling silver and 18-karat gold bimetal; hammer textured, pierced, formed, oxidized

PHOTO BY RALPH GABRINER

Biba Schutz

Lacy Loops | 2005

EACH, 4.4 X 4.4 X 1.8 CM

Sterling silver, 22-karat gold; cast, forged, hand fabricated, oxidized

PHOTO BY RON BOSZKO
COURTESY OF OBJECTS OF DESIRE ART GALLERY, LOUISVILLE, KENTUCKY

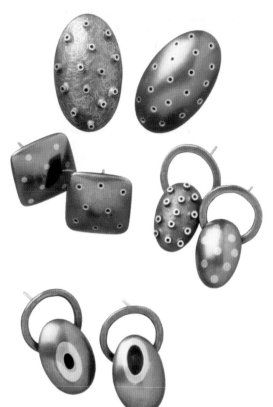

Catherine Hills
Group from the series
Earrings for an Odd Moment | 1999
LARGEST, 3.5 CM; SMALLEST, 2 CM
Silver, 18-karat yellow gold; hand
fabricated, pressed, inlay, oxidized
PHOTO BY NORMAN HOLLANDS

Julie Jerman-Melka
Flora/Fauna Earrings | 2005
EACH, 3 X 1 X 0.3 CM
Sterling silver, 18-karat gold, yellow
sapphires, patina; hand hammered,
fabricated, forged, granulation, tube set
PHOTO BY HAP SAKWA

Patricia Tschetter
Process II | 2006
EACH, 3.2 X 2.5 X 1 CM
Sterling silver, 18-karat gold, 24-karat gold, patina; hand
fabricated, kum boo, soldered, cold connected, oxidized
PHOTO BY ROBERT DIAMANTE

Dolores Barrett
Sundial Earrings | 2006
EACH, 6.2 X 1.5 X 2 CM
Dichroic and art glass, gold-filled
wire; fused, hand polished
PHOTO BY ARTIST

*This set is designed to be inserted
from behind the ear and is coun-
terbalanced with the iridized glass
"suns" in front. Each round "sun"
piece has an embedded rubber stop-
per to hold the wire
finding securely.* DOLORES BARRETT

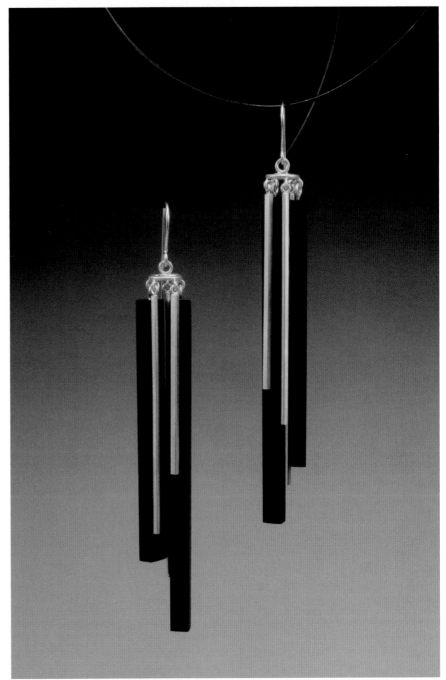

Julia Turner
Untitled | 2006
EACH, 8 X 1 X 1 CM
Ebony, 18-karat gold
PHOTO BY ARTIST

Contributing Artists

AALUND, NANZ Waukesha, Wisconsin 167, 374
ABRASHA San Francisco, California 73, 156, 270
ACOSTA, CHERYLEVE Mesilla Park, New Mexico 161, 243, 365
AL QUBAISI, AZZA Abu Dhabi, United Arab Emirates 376, 387
ALBURG, MAREEN Halle, Germany 13
ALONSO, VERÓNICA Buenos Aires, Argentina 240
AMANO, SHIHOKO Wallkill, New York 77, 286
ANDERSON, BRUCE Stanfordville, New York 369
ARAGON, LAURA El Paso, Texas 327
ARAI, CHIEKO Cedar Rapids, Iowa 186
ARENAS, ELIANA R. Las Cruces, New Mexico 30, 119
ATAUMBI, KERI Santa Fe, New Mexico 106, 108
ATKINS, W. TAFT Springfield, Missouri 370
AUMAN, MEGAN Jonestown, Pennsylvania 346
BABIKIAN, HRATCH Philadelphia, Pennsylvania 298, 355
BACHMANN, KAREN Brooklyn, New York 90
BAKER, SANDY New York, New York 114, 316
BANEHAM, JESSICA Whitby, Canada 250
BARELLO, JULIA Las Cruces, New Mexico 79
BARER, BELLE BROOKE Los Angeles, California 265
BARK, MIJIN Seoul, Korea 59
BARON, DIANNE KARG Oshawa, Canada 135
BARRETT, DOLORES Camarillo, California 337, 404
BASHAROVA, NINA New York, New York 261, 372
BAUER, CECELIA New York, New York 141, 304
BAUSER, JENNIFER Seattle, Washington 245, 260
BAUSMAN, DAVID Laredo, Texas 358
BAYNE, BARBARA Montague, Massachusetts 170, 204
BEHRENDS, JULIA Boston, Massachusetts 208
BENSINGER, CAROLYN Watertown, Massachusetts 380, 391
BERSANI, CLAIRE New York, New York 74
BIGAZZI, DAVIDE San Diego, California 285
BIGKNIFE, HEIDI Tulsa, Oklahoma 178, 366
BIRD, CHELSEA E. Oakton, Virginia 134
BOISVERT, LAURIE Port Joli, Canada 129
BOLHUIS, KRISTINE Ferndale, Michigan 48, 344, 385
BONE, ELIZABETH London, England 272
BROTHERTON, TIFFANY Springfield, Missouri 342
BUBASH, ANGELA Penland, North Carolina 29
BUONGIOVANNI, MONICA Florence, Italy 187
BURKHOLDER, AMY Waconia, Minnesota 389
CALUM, K.C. Basking Ridge, New Jersey 249, 303, 332
CANNON, AMY Troy, New York 361, 364
CARLSON, CHRIS Deland, Florida 192
CARNAT, SARABETH Calgary, Canada 380
CATCHPOLE, BRIDGET Vancouver, Canada 55, 325
CHACHENIAN, JENNIFER W. North Providence, Rhode Island 224, 290
CHAN, MICHELLE Richmond Hill, Canada 239
CHANG, YUYEN Madison, Wisconsin 105
CHAVENT, CLAUDE Puechabon, France 6, 169, 270
CHAVENT, FRANÇOISE Puechabon, France 6, 169, 270
CHEN, WALTER Barcelona, Spain 185
CHERVITZ, RANDI S. Saint Louis, Missouri 241
CHESICK, EMILY Minneapolis, Minnesota 39
CHIA-PEI, HSIAO Tainan, Taiwan 85, 343
CHIU, CHIH-WEN Tainan, Taiwan 363
CHOTARD, CATHY Montpellier, France 61, 359
CHRISTIANSEN, LYNN San Francisco, California 177, 196, 197
CLASS, PETRA San Francisco, California 208
CLAUSAGER, KIRSTEN Vanløse, Denmark 174, 211, 347
CLOSE, DOUGLAS Oceanside, California 359
COBB-TAPPAN, SHANNON Dunedin, Florida 95
CODDENS, LAURA Bristol, Indiana 229, 281
COGSWELL, JOHN Clintondale, New York 80
COHEN, JIM Madison, Wisconsin 112

COHEN, BARBARA Vancouver, Canada 56, 284, 302
COOK, OCTAVIA Kingsland, New Zealand 283
COONEN, LUANA Oakland, California 26, 137
COOPER, DELANE Toronto, Canada 378
CORVAJA, GIOVANNI Todi, Italy 13, 155, 261, 263
CORYELL, RONDA Oakland, California 144, 258, 396
COSTA, CLAUDIA Siena, Italy 68, 124
COUNARD, CAPPY Edinboro, Pennsylvania 164
COZZI, LOUISE FISCHER Brooklyn, New York 193
CRAIG, GABRIEL Kalamazoo, Michigan 220
CRAMPSIE, DANIELLE Toronto, Canada 242
CRESPO, PAULA Lisbon, Portugal 377
CROWDER, LISA Austin, Texas 348
DABROWSKI, MARYA Providence, Rhode Island 41, 138
DAEGER, POLLY Milwaukee, Wisconsin 96, 387
DAHER, DEBORRAH St. Louis, Missouri 76
DANSEREAU, LAURIE Montreal, Canada 104, 383
DAVEY, CAITLYN Portland, Oregon 53
DAVIES, JESSICA San Francisco, California 233
DEAN, TAMI Portland, Oregon 75, 142, 149, 206, 395
DEANS, REBECCA San Francisco, California 248
DEBUS, LAUREN Austin, Texas 277
DECKERS, PETER Upper Hutt, New Zealand 89
DESJARDINS, JOSÉE Canton-de-Hatley, Canada 383
DHEIN, CHRISTINE San Francisco, California 52, 166, 310
DIRESTA, KATHLEEN Sea Cliff, New York 204
DONIVAN, JO-ANN MAGGIORA San Francisco, California 139
DONIVAN, JOHN Oakland, California 254
DUDEK, DIANA Munich, Germany 190
DUNCAN, DEREK MCKAY San Francisco, California 25, 271
DUPONT, NADIA MORGENTHALER St. Julien-en-Genevois, France 328, 363
EHINGER, ANNETTE Pforzheim, Germany 6, 36, 136
EID, CYNTHIA Lexington, Massachusetts 309
EISMANN, BEATE Halle, Germany 81, 121
ELLISON-DORION, HELEN El Paso, Texas 98, 236
ESK, GLEN Stokenchurch, England 353
ESSER, SUZANNE Amstelveen, Netherlands 218, 269
FERRERO, TOM Bloomington, Indiana 198
FETTER, PEG St. Louis, Missouri 386
FONTAINE, LORETTA Albany, New York 37, 336
FONTANA, VENEZIA Huerth, Germany 169
FONTANS, DEE Calgary, Canada 340
FOSTER, JESSICA Richmond, Virginia 128
FREIER, CHRISTOPH Keitum, Germany 397
FRIEDMAN, GAYLE Washington, D.C. 191
GARGIULO, FLORENCIA Buenos Aires, Argentina 384
GELTMAN, ELIZABETH GLASS Washington, D.C. 226
GERSTEIN, EILEEN San Rafael, California 94
GILBERTSON, CATHERINE CLARK Madison, Wisconsin 7, 64, 318
GILES, GEOFFREY D. Candler, North Carolina 50, 262, 315
GOOD, MICHAEL Rockport, Maine 8, 154
GOODMAN, JOYCE New York, New York 195
GOSSEN, BARBI Kent, Ohio 231
GOTTLIEB, LORI MEG Owings Mills, Maryland 107
GRAFTON, ADRIENNE M. Penland, North Carolina 202
GRZYB, JANICE New York, New York 74
GUIDERO, HEATHER Providence, Rhode Island 253
HAGA, LEE RAMSEY Portland, Oregon 165, 200, 357
HANAWA, NORIKO Chiba, Japan 97
HANNON, REBECCA Ithaca, New York 87
HARRELL, JAN ARTHUR Houston, Texas 164
HATTORI, YOSHIE Vancouver, Canada 338
HEBIB, MIA Brooklyn, New York 160
HEINDL, ANNA Vienna, Austria 210, 252, 379
HEINRICH, BARBARA Pittsford, New York 152, 216
HENTZ, CHRISTOPHER A. Baton Rouge, Louisiana 66, 395
HERMAN, THOMAS Stone Ridge, New York 265, 374
HERNANDEZ, JONATHAN Littlefield, Texas 110, 158, 317

Herynek, Pavel Olomouc, Czech Republic 120, 294
Higashi, April Berkeley, California 54
Hills, Catherine London, England 402
Himic, Ellen Cherryville, Pennsylvania 3, 288
Hipólito, Leonor Lisbon, Portugal 122, 129
Ho, Charmaine San Francisco, California 125, 369
Hood, Sarah Seattle, Washington 236
Hosom, Dorothea Falmouth, Massachusetts 274
Hovey-King, Cuyler Fayetteville, Georgia 111
Hu, Mary Lee Seattle, Washington 14, 213
Hüebner, Bettina Berlin, Germany 397
Hung, Angela K. Carlinville, Illinois 57
Hylands, Catherine San Francisco, California 173
Ishiyama, Reiko New York, New York 173, 269, 401
Jackson, Rob Athens, Georgia 21, 200, 354
Jackson, Debbie Columbus, Ohio 132
Jacobi, Jessica The Woodlands, Texas 278
Jacobson, Hadar Berkeley, California 366
Jennings, Jack Asheville, North Carolina 308
Jerman-Melka, Julie Fort Collins, Colorado 297, 402
Jestin, Marty Palmerston North, New Zealand 181
Johnson, Tracy Harpswell, Maine 143
Juhasz, Jackie Manitou Beach, Michigan 330
Jun, Hu Beijing, China 117, 222
Kamata, Jiro Munich, Germany 113, 159
Kanazawa, Mark Chicago, Illinois 18, 69
Kanner, Dahlia Charlestown, Rhode Island 393
Kaphan, Jeffrey Jackson, Wyoming 146, 391
Kataoka, Masumi Denton, Texas 127
Kato, Karin Tokyo, Japan 246
Kawai, Satomi Iowa City, Iowa 91
Kaya, James Boston, Massachusetts 375
Keeney, Brent R. Juneau, Alaska 255, 335
Kerman, Janis Westmount, Canada 45, 207
Kern, Tamar Newport, Rhode Island 211
Kim, Wanjin Gainesville, Virginia 32
Kim, Eun Mi Seoul, South Korea 163, 349
Kim, Sun Kyoung Champaign, Illinois 107
Klockmann, Beate Amsterdam, Netherlands 46
Ko, Hyejeong Seoul, South Korea 28, 351
Kolb, Giselle Laurel, Maryland 33
Kovalcik, Terry Haledon, New Jersey 203, 253
Kovel, Kathy Oakland, California 94, 143
Krinos, Daphne London, England 51, 93, 345
Kukuchek, Anna San Diego, California 82
Kumagai, Cindy San Francisco, California 179
Kupke-Peyla, Birgit Salinas, California 61
Lachowiec, Tricia New Bedford, Massachusetts 381
Laken, Birgit Haarlem, Netherlands 105
Lamb, Hannah Louise Edinburgh, Scotland 88, 289
LaPenne, Katrina Brooklyn, New York 279
Lauseng, Karen J. Silver City, New Mexico 191, 295, 337
Lavrovsky, Vlad Los Angeles, California 42
Leathers, Paul Red Deer, Canada 396
Lederman, Lulu Providence, Rhode Island 341
Lee, Sungyeoul Champaign, Illinois 183, 339
Leicht, Hans-Erwin Matadepera, Spain 227
Leister, Kyle H. Staunton, Virginia 199
Lemon, Christina Statesboro, Georgia 36
Lewton-Brain, Charles Calgary, Canada 62, 67
Lim, Cesar Los Angeles, California 42
Lippe, Micki Seattle, Washington 80, 333, 373
Longyear, Robert St. Louis, Missouri 276
Lorich, Anna Providence, Rhode Island 125
Lubin, Laura Newtonville, Massachusetts 389
Lühtje, Christa Stockdorf, Germany 58
Luttin, Sim Bloomington, Indiana 245
MacBain, Kenneth Morristown, New Jersey 386
Maierhofer, Fritz Vienna, Austria 303
Maljojoki, Mia Munich, Germany 324, 326
Massey, Sharon Greenville, North Carolina 19
Mattioli New Rochelle, New York 73
McCreary, Karen Long Beach, California 227
McKim, Betty Raleigh, North Carolina 367
McLoughlin, Emily Carrollton, Texas 225
Melnick, Dana Holmdel, New Jersey 219
Minor, Barbara Baton Rouge, Louisiana 395
Mitchell, Karen, Karen Mitchell Design Aspen, Colorado 21, 259
Mitchelhill, Noon London, England 24
Moscow, Mi-Mi Moscow, Russia 83
Murphy Design Minneapolis, Minnesota 39
Myers, Paulette Collinsville, Illinois 315
Nahabetian, Dennis Orchard Park, New York 60, 212
Nassiri, Neda New York, New York 357
Neubauer, Ben Portland, Oregon 49, 175
Newbrook, Jill London, England 167, 393
Nichols, Kerstin Hartford, Vermont 352
Noakes, Kristin Halifax, Canada 224
Nowlan, Michelle Arlington, Massachusetts 132
Ochoa V., Maria Constanza Florence, Italy 118
Oguro, Yuzuka Kanagawa, Japan 233
Onodera, Masako Urbana, Illinois 35, 130
Orbanic, Kelly A. Johnstown, Colorado 100
Osgood, Kathryn Wanchese, North Carolina 394
Oye, Emiko San Francisco, California 182
Pagliai, Mariel Montreal, Canada 320
Pankowski, Gina Seattle, Washington 27, 392
Pantelidou, Silina, Athens, Greece 234
Papac, Seth Everett, Washington 174
Park, Jun Seoul, Korea 103
Parkin, Ann Rye Brook, New York 367
paterak, j.e. Westbrook, Maine 175
Pavlov, Dmitriy Madison, Wisconsin 209
Payer, Jeanine San Francisco, California 115
Penny, Sarah Toronto, Canada 115
Perrino, Leslie Racine, Wisconsin 176, 188
Peters, Jan Lexington, Kentucky 162, 207
Petersen, Stacy Attleboro, Massachusetts 360, 382
Peterson, Lina London, England 116
Pham, Rosemary Seattle, Washington 272
Pressey, Bronwyn Jayne Redfern, Australia 362
Preston, Mary Brooklyn, New York 221
Prindiville, Kathleen R. Warren, Rhode Island 123
Redman, Jayne Cumberland, Maine 17, 267
Reed, Todd Boulder, Colorado 47, 214, 313
Reed, Madeline Arcadia, Kansas 235
Reihberg, Cara Sydney, Australia 182
Revere, Alan San Francisco, California 65, 157, 296
Revere, Dustin Berkeley, California 388
Rice, Lyndsay Milwaukee, Wisconsin 184
Rickard, Tessa E. Hamtramck, Michigan 34
Rinn, Kari Richmond, Virginia 50
Robertson, Kaz Edinburgh, Scotland 229
Roitzsch, Antje Rockport, Maine 259
Romeo, Alexis Webster, New York 99
Rooker, Mark Harrisonburg, Virginia 189
Rosengard, Beth Los Angeles, California 145, 153, 311
Rust, Vina Seattle, Washington 400
Ruth, Glenda Oakland, California 201, 399
Ryan, Jacqueline Todi, Italy 10, 63, 172
Saito, Yuka New York, New York 246, 300
Sajet, Philip Amsterdam, Netherlands 279
Sakamoto, Eddie Torrance, California 43, 70, 323
Samuels, Sasha Portland, Oregon 310, 322
Sangra, Kiren Niki Grande Prairie, Canada 301
Sarah Graham Metalsmithing La Quinta, California 314

SARDAMOV, NIKOLAY Sofia, Bulgaria 232
SAWYER, GEORGE Minneapolis, Minnesota 264, 321
SCAVEZZE, JERRY Salida, Colorado 13, 217, 256
SCHICK, MARJORIE Pittsburg, Kansas 293
SCHMITZ, CLAUDE Luxembourg 40, 251
SCHUTZ, BIBA New York, New York 282, 401
SCOFIELD, JESSICA Missoula, Montana 5, 266
SHERMAN, SONDRA Dorchester, Massachusetts 20
SHIMAZU, DONNA E. Kailua, Hawaii 280
SHIMIZU, YOKO Florence, Italy 280
SHIN, HYESEUNG Chicago, Illinois 275
SILLS, CHERYL Mission Bay, New Zealand 342
SILVERMAN, SUMNER Tisbury, Massachusetts 304
SIMON, MARJORIE Highland Park, New Jersey 237, 292, 371
SKRODER, LARS Lauderdale-by-the-Sea, Florida 168
SMILEY, NISA Sullivan, Maine 106
SMITH, JESSEE J. Cincinnati, Ohio 31, 234
SMITH, LULU Seattle, Washington 31
SOBER, JULIA CONVERSE DeKalb, Illinois 193
SPECKNER, BETTINA Ubersee, Germany 376
SPIES, KLAUS Chicago, Illinois 171
SUGAWARA, NORIKO New York, New York 7, 9, 16
TAI, LEILA New York, New York 147, 207
TANAKA, YAS Oakland, California 44
TANCHAROEN, RUDEE Florence, Italy 223
TANIELIAN, VASKEN San Francisco, California 368
TEIPEL, MARCUS Barcelona, Spain 140
TENENBAUM, JOAN Gig Harbor, Washington 258
THIBADO, KEN Boonville, New York 178
THIEWES, RACHELLE El Paso, Texas 244
TOKOLY, ELIZABETH ANN Jersey City, New Jersey 331
TSCHETTER, PATRICIA Dallas, Texas 72, 403
TURNER, JULIA San Francisco, California 405
UEMURA, CHRISTINE Pacheco, California 22
UPIN, MUNYA AVIGAIL Belmont, Massachusetts 194, 241
VAN ASWEGEN, JOHAN Providence, Rhode Island 93, 126, 247
VAN DER LEEST, FELIEKE Amsterdam, Netherlands 230
VAN DER VEGTE, MAARTEN Almere, Netherlands 109
VANDAMME, INGEBORG Amsterdam, Netherlands 99
VENALECK, PATRICIA ZABRESKI Macomb, Michigan 329
VERBEEK, MIRIAM El Zutphen, Netherlands 350
VINCENT, DIANA Washington Crossing, Pennsylvania 40, 71
VON DOHNANYI, BABETTE Florence, Italy 162
WAINWRIGHT, JENNA New York, New York 287, 291
WALES, POLLY East Molesey, England 151
WALKER, GRETCHEN San Francisco, California 101
WANG, KIWON New York, New York 38
WANG-BISHOP, GRACE Prospect Heights, Illinois 43
WEAVER, SEAN Elmira, New York 148, 215
WEAVER, SCOTT Elmira, New York 148, 215
WEBB, CAROL Santa Cruz, California 205
WEHRENS, JAN Munich, Germany 92
WEIKS, AMY Kalamazoo, Michigan 240
WEISENBURG, ROBERTA ANN San Francisco, California 260
WERNER, WAYNE Havre de Grace, Maryland 306, 373
WHITE, STEPHANIE Marietta, Georgia 131
WIK, JOHN Winona, Minnesota 274
WILBANKS, SARAH Seattle, Washington 295
WISE, JEFF Durango, Colorado 305, 390, 398
WISE, SUSAN Durango, Colorado 305, 390, 398
WOLF, KATE Portland, Maine 307
WOZNIAK, NATASHA New York, New York 11, 257
WU, HSUEH-YING Tainan, Taiwan 86
WU, SHU-LIN Taipei, Taiwan 133
YAMADA, MIZUKO Tokyo, Japan 273
YAMAMOTO, YOSHIKO Boston, Massachusetts 268
YANG, HEA JIN Yeonwon, South Korea 180
YEATS, KATHRYN KHARDALLAH Wellington, New Zealand 350

YEN, LIAUNG-CHUNG Rochester, New York 215, 319
YI, JENNIFER Brooklyn, New York 356
YOKOUCHI, SAYUMI Brooklyn, New York 150
YOON, JAE SEUNG Seoul, Korea 23
YU-FANG, CHI Tainan, Taiwan 238
ZABALA, IZASKUN Brooklyn, New York 299
ZANELLA, ANNAMARIA Padua, Italy 12, 84, 312
ZAPPELLINI, MAUREEN BRUSA Tucson, Arizona 102
ZITSERMAN, RUSLANA Rego Park, New York 194

Acknowledgments

This exceptional collection is a tribute to Alan Revere's passion for jewelry and his inimitable knowledge of design, technique, and history. We feel extremely fortunate to have worked with him. His enthusiasm for jewelry is matched only by his energetic and generous spirit, attributes that made the long and intense jurying deliberations a pleasure.

We are deeply appreciative of all of the jewelers who submitted images for this publication. Without their willingness to share their talent with Lark Books and its readers, we could never have created this book. We are consistently amazed and inspired by their imagination, innovation, and dedication to the medium.

A warm thank you to the galleries, guilds, and schools that vigorously promote and enrich the field of studio jewelry. They contributed immeasurably to disseminating information about this book and to ensuring the volume of submissions we received.

We're indebted to our first-rate editorial assistants—Dawn Dillingham, Delores Gosnell, and Rosemary Kast. Their careful attention to detail kept the process smooth and on track. Thanks to art department assistants Shannon Yokeley and Lance Wille for their steadfast support during the book's production. Thank you to Matt Shay for his consummate design; we couldn't ask for a better showcase for the jewelry. And finally, we are grateful for the superb work of Janet Hurley, an editor and writer of tremendous skill.

This book is dedicated to Nathalie Mornu—a champion collaborator, inquisitive intellect, sounding board, reality check, tireless supporter, and friend.

Marthe Le Van